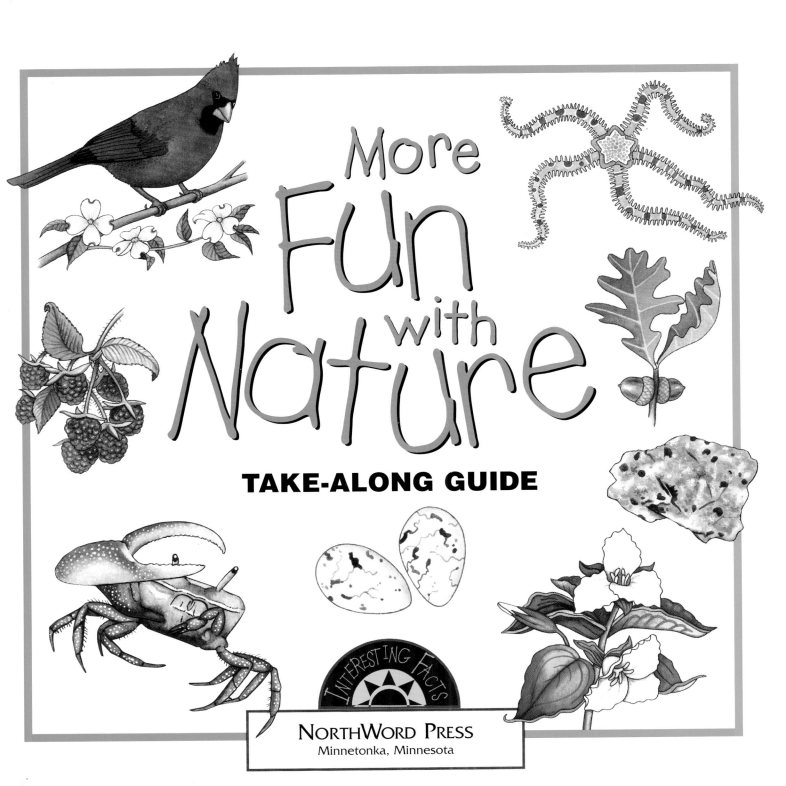

More Fun with Nature

TAKE-ALONG GUIDE

INTERESTING FACTS

NORTHWORD PRESS
Minnetonka, Minnesota

NorthWord Press
5900 Green Oak Drive
Minnetonka, MN 55343
1-800-328-3895
www.northwordpress.com

Library of Congress Cataloging-in-Publication Data
More fun with nature : take-along guide.
    p. cm.
      Contents: 1. Berries, nuts and seeds / by Diane L. Burns, illustrations by John F. McGee. -- 2. Birds, nests and eggs / by Mel Boring, illustrations by Linda Garrow. -- 3. Wildflowers, blooms and blossoms / by Diane L. Burns, illustrations by Linda Garrow. -- 4. Rocks, fossils and arrowheads / by Laura Evert, illustrations by Linda Garrow. -- 5. Seashells, crabs and sea stars / by Christiane Kump Tibbitts, illustrations by Linda Garrow.
      ISBN 1-55971-795-5 (hardcover)
      1. Animals--Juvenile literature. 2. Plants--Juvenile literature. [1. Animals. 2. Plants. 3. Nature.] 1. NorthWord Press.

QL49 .M796 2001
578--dc21   2001032648

Printed in Singapore
10 9 8 7 6 5 4 3 2 1

More Fun with Nature

TAKE-ALONG GUIDE

Berries, Nuts and Seeds
by Diane L. Burns
illustrations by John F. McGee

Birds, Nests and Eggs
by Mel Boring
illustrations by Linda Garrow

Rocks, Fossils and Arrowheads
by Laura Evert
illustrations by Linda Garrow

Seashells, Crabs and Sea Stars
by Christiane Kump Tibbitts
illustrations by Linda Garrow

Wildflowers, Blooms and Blossoms
by Diane L. Burns
illustrations by Linda Garrow

Contents

Berries, Nuts and Seeds

DEDICATION
To my dear daughter-in-law, Jill, who knows that everything grows with love.

ACKNOWLEDGMENTS
Many thanks to the following people for assisting in the research and proofreading of this manuscript:
The Rhinelander District Library, especially Cheryle Miller. Rhinelander High School botany teacher Dawn Bassuener.
Central Elementary School teachers Tom Doyle and Joyce Minks. Consolidated Paper Company forester Dan Hartman.
Chequamegon National Forest wildlife biologist Norm Weiland. Field experts (and berry lovers) Robin and Jerry Burns,
Bill and Barb Goosman, and Clint and Jill Burns.

Contents

DEDICATION
For Katy, my daughter and research assistant, with love.

ACKNOWLEDGMENTS
I am grateful to Rita Hirv, Librarian of the Rockford, Iowa, Public Library, and Marilyn Buttjer, Children's Librarian at the Charles City, Iowa, Public Library. They have helped a lot to make this book, probably without even realizing it.

Contents

Rocks, Fossils and Arrowheads

DEDICATION
For Olivia Bruni,
whose world of exploration and discovery
is just beginning.

Contents

Seashells, Crabs and Sea Stars

DEDICATION
For my parents, who first showed me the wonders of the ocean

ACKNOWLEDGMENTS
My heartfelt thanks go to Cristy Mittelstadt, Environmental Educator at the North Carolina Aquarium at Pine Knoll Shores for her suggestions and scientific review of the manuscript; to other Aquarium staff for their help; to Hugh Porter, Curator of Collections, University of North Carolina Institute of Marine Sciences, for answering questions; to Consie Powell and Marnie Brooks for editing and proofreading help; to my family—Dean, Alexandra and Veronica—for their untiring support; to Diane Burns for cheering me on; to the Apex Public Library staff, Pamela Marino of the Cousteau Society, and Merrill Manke of the Monterey Bay Aquarium for graciously helping me obtain research materials.

Contents

Wildflowers, Blooms and Blossoms

DEDICATION

To my nieces, Heather, Amanda and Kelly, three lovely flowers of young womanhood. Bloom and flourish, dear hearts.

ACKNOWLEDGMENTS

Grateful thanks to Rhinelander High School botany teacher, Dawn Bassuener; at Hanson's Rhinelander Floral Company, Karen Stroede; Jill Burns, Karen Sackett, Bonnie Kofler and especially the Hempels—Ruth and Henning—of Forth Floral.

Take-Along Guide

Berries, Nuts and Seeds

by Diane L. Burns   illustrations by John F. McGee

INTRODUCTION

Berries, nuts and seeds are actually the fruits of many kinds of plants. They come in many shapes and sizes and usually ripen near the end of summer. Most provide important food for different kinds of animals. Some, but not all, can also be eaten by people.

Depending on the kind of plant, its fruit may be juicy, or tough, or have hard shells. Usually, an outer covering protects the fruit from heat and cold, too much or too little moisture, and other dangers.

Plants protect their fruit in other ways, too. They may grow spines and thorns. They may taste bad or be poisonous. They may hang out of reach.

Berries, nuts and seeds can fall to the ground and begin to grow. They might also travel and start new plants far away. Some are blown by the wind. Some ride piggyback by sticking to fur or to skin. Some even roll along the ground.

This Take-Along Guide and its activities will help you find some of the interesting things growing on plants, trees and bushes. You can use the ruler on the back cover to measure what you discover. You can bring a pencil and draw what you see in the Scrapbook.

Have fun exploring the world of Berries, Nuts and Seeds!

WINTERGREEN

WHAT IT LOOKS LIKE

Wintergreen is a short, creeping plant with a stiff stem. It grows from 4 to 6 inches tall.

The oval leaves are thick and leathery. They are dark green and shiny on top. The leaves grow from 1 to 2 inches long.

Wintergreen flowers are tiny, white and look like little bells.

The berry is the size of a pea and bright pink-red. It looks and feels waxy. Wintergreen berries ripen in autumn and stay on the plant all winter.

WHERE TO FIND IT

In dry, shady places look under large shrubs and pine trees. Look along roadsides, too.

In summer, look for the white flower. In autumn and winter, look for the bright pink-red berry.

Wintergreen grows in the eastern states and as far south as Georgia. It also grows in the north-central United States, west to Minnesota.

WHAT EATS IT

Wintergreen berries are food for partridge, grouse, deer, mice and bears.

12

Tell an adult where you are going, or take one with you!

JUNIPER

WHAT IT LOOKS LIKE

Some junipers grow as a low shrub only a few feet tall. Junipers can also be short trees up to 40 feet tall. The bark is red-brown. Some kinds of juniper bark are soft and look shredded. Other kinds are thin.

Some juniper leaves are needle-like and grow less than 1 inch long. Others are even shorter and scaly. They lay flat against the twig.

The berry is really a cone of plump scales. It is round and less than 1/2 inch across. It is green in spring and turns blue-black as it ripens in September and October.

WHERE TO FIND IT

Look for junipers on dry, rocky soil where other trees could not easily grow. They also grow on hillsides and in fields.

In winter, look for the blue-black berries still hanging on the branches.

Junipers are found from New England across the Midwest and south to Georgia, and from Texas into the southwestern states and north into the Rocky Mountains.

WHAT EATS IT

Many kinds of wildlife eat juniper berries including turkeys, pheasants, quail, cardinals, robins, waxwings, finches, and woodpeckers. Mice, chipmunks, opossums, foxes and antelope also eat juniper berries.

Get permission before going onto someone else's land.

CRANBERRY

WHAT IT LOOKS LIKE

Cranberry plants grow from 3 to 6 inches tall. They grow on a creeping, woody vine. The plants look like a mat across the ground.

The green leaves are smaller than your fingernail. They are oval and tough.

Cranberry flowers are small, drooping, and pink-white. They bloom in May and June.

The oval berries are the size of marbles. The unripe fruit is green. It turns bright red in September and October.

WHAT EATS IT

Cranes and grouse eat cranberries. So do bears and deer. People eat cranberries, too.

WHERE TO FIND IT

Cranberries grow where there is lots of sunshine. Look in open edges along road-sides and wet places.

Cranberries grow from Massachusetts south to North Carolina and west into Minnesota. They also grow in Washington and Oregon.

Watch where you step.

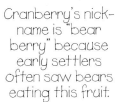

INTERESTING FACTS

Cranberry's nickname is "bear berry" because early settlers often saw bears eating this fruit.

More than 400 million pounds of cranberries are harvested every year in North America.

BUNCHBERRY

WHAT IT LOOKS LIKE

Bunchberries are green plants that grow from 3 to 8 inches tall.

Near the top of the stem, 4 to 6 oval leaves grow in a circle. They are lime-green and smooth. They are about 2 1/2 inches long. Each leaf has deep lines.

Light green bunchberry flowers grow in a tiny cluster. The cluster is at the center of the leaves. The flowers bloom in May.

Ripe bunchberries are red and round. They hang in a small cluster from the center of the leaves. Each fruit is about the size of a small pea. The fruit is ripe in June and July.

WHERE TO FIND IT

Bunchberries grow in cool, shady places. Look for the circle of leaves around the stem.

Bunchberries grow from Maine to West Virginia. They are also found across northern New England and the Great Lakes states, and from Washington east to Montana, and south to the mountains in California.

WHAT EATS IT

Bunchberries are eaten by grouse, robins and sparrows.

INTERESTING FACTS

Its name comes from the tiny cluster of red fruit that hangs from the plant in summer.

Ripe bunchberries can be used as bait for minnows.

A hat with a brim will protect you from sunburn.

BAYBERRY

WHAT IT LOOKS LIKE

Bayberry is a shrub. It can grow to about 40 feet tall, but it is usually much shorter. The branches are stiff, gray and waxy.

The stiff bayberry leaves stick upright and are shiny and tough. They grow about 3 inches long and about 1 inch wide.

Some bayberry flowers look like caterpillars. They bloom in spring.

The small, waxy berries are gray-green or pale blue. They look like tiny beads and are smaller than 1/4 inch. They ripen in early autumn. They stay on the bush all winter.

WHAT EATS IT

Quail, swallows and vireos eat bayberries. So do foxes. Deer eat the leaves and stems.

WHERE TO FIND IT

Bayberries grow in moist places, like swamps. Wear boots when you are exploring for them.

Bayberry grows across New England and along the East Coast.

16

Be sure you show any berries to an adult before eating them.

SERVICEBERRY

WHAT IT LOOKS LIKE

Some kinds of serviceberry are shrubs. Some are trees that grow to more than 40 feet tall. The bark is streaked green-gray when it is young. It is furrowed into ridges on older trees.

The oval leaves are shiny and light green with little "teeth" on the edges. The leaves are about 3 inches long.

The white flowers hang in drooping clusters. They open in April or May. The petals are thin and less than 1/2 inch long with yellow centers.

Serviceberry fruit is small and round—about the size of a marble. It is green to red when it is unripe, and becomes purple-black and hard. The fruit looks like a tiny apple with a dry, red "star" at the bottom. It ripens in June.

WHERE TO FIND IT

Serviceberries like dry, sunny places. They grow in clumps on hillsides, above stream banks and in dry woods.

Serviceberries grow throughout the United States, except for parts of California, Texas, Oklahoma, and the Gulf Coast.

WHAT EATS IT

Grouse, crows, thrushes and tanagers eat these berries. Bears and squirrels do, too. Rabbits, marmots and deer eat the bark and twigs as well as the berries.

Do not pick berries that grow along heavily traveled roads. They could be polluted.

SPECIAL WARNING

CURRANT

WHAT IT LOOKS LIKE

Currants grow on a bush or shrub that is from 4 to 6 feet tall. Some currant bushes have thorns. Others do not.

The green leaves grow up to 3 inches long. They have 3 to 5 big dents on the edges.

Currant flowers look like stars. They grow in drooping clusters and bloom in May. Up to 10 small flowers grow in a clump. They can be green, pink, yellow or red.

The berries are round and the size of peas. They have a papery brown "pigtail" hanging from the bottom. There are up to 10 berries in a cluster. They can be red, white or black.

WHERE TO FIND IT

Currants grow in sunny spots and in moist places near water. Look along creeks and streams. They also grow on rocky hillsides.

Different types of currants grow throughout the United States.

WHAT EATS IT

Currant berries are eaten by catbirds and robins. Chipmunks and ground squirrels eat them, too. So do some people. Hummingbirds like the flowers.

Wear long pants and a long-sleeved shirt to protect yourself from thorns and insects.

18

SUMAC

Sumac grows on rocky ground. Look for it on open hillsides, edges of trails, grasslands and along roadsides.

WHAT IT LOOKS LIKE

Sumac can grow over 20 feet tall. Some sumacs have thick, hairy branches that twist. Others have smooth branches. The bark is dark brown-gray.

Different types of sumac grow throughout the United States.

Most kinds of sumac have narrow leaflets about 4 to 6 inches long. They have teeth on the edges and are whitish underneath.

The yellow-green flowers grow in clusters. They bloom in June and July. Each small flower has 5 petals.

WHAT EATS IT

The fuzzy berries are green and ripen to dark red. Each berry is the size of a small, flat pea. They grow in clusters about as long as your hand. The cluster looks like an upside-down cone.

Sumac berries are eaten by bluebirds, cardinals, thrushes and wild turkeys. Rabbits and chipmunks eat them, too.

INTERESTING FACTS

One type of sumac, the "staghorn," gets its name from the velvety twigs that look like deer antlers.

Stay away from sumacs that grow in wet places and have smooth, white berries—they are poisonous!

SPECIAL WARNING

19

GOOSEBERRY

WHAT IT LOOKS LIKE

Gooseberry shrubs grow from 3 to 5 feet tall. The stems grow every which way.

Gooseberry leaves are about 1 inch wide and 3 inches long. They have 3 to 5 large dents and large teeth on the edges. The green leaves are stiff.

The flowers grow in groups of 1 to 3 and bloom in April and May. They are small and shaped like a bell, and can be green, white, yellow or purple.

The berries grow in clusters of 1 to 3. The skin can be smooth or hairy. They ripen in late July and August. Ripe gooseberries can be green, pink or brown-purple. Some types have light colored stripes from top to bottom.

WHERE TO FIND IT

Gooseberries grow on wooded hillsides and dry ditches. They also grow in open woods.

Gooseberries are found from New England south to the Gulf Coast. Also, westward across the Plains and the Rocky Mountains into the Pacific Northwest.

WHAT EATS IT

Hummingbirds like gooseberry flowers. Blue jays, chipmunks, skunks and mice eat the fruit. People eat gooseberries, too.

INTERESTING FACTS

The bottom of the gooseberry is really the top. The brown "pigtail" is what is left of the flower.

Gooseberries usually have thorns on the stems, especially near the branches.

RASPBERRY

WHAT IT LOOKS LIKE

Bushy raspberry plants grow 4 to 6 feet tall. The stems are thick and have prickles on them.

Red raspberry stems are brownish. Young black raspberry stems are green-blue. Older ones are red.

Raspberry leaves are medium green. They are silver-white underneath and about the length of your finger.

The flowers bloom in June and July in clusters of white or pink blossoms. They have 5 petals. The flowers are less than 1 inch wide.

Each raspberry fruit looks like a tiny round igloo. It is about the size of your fingertip. The fruit is green before it ripens to bright red or purple-black. Raspberries are ripe in July and August.

WHERE TO FIND IT

These berries like sunshine. Raspberries often grow in a thick tangle on the edges of woods, meadows and roadsides.

Raspberries grow across the northeastern and central United States and west into the Rocky Mountains.

WHAT EATS IT

Robins, bluebirds, flycatchers, sparrows, thrushes, pheasants, cardinals, catbirds and quails eat raspberries. Bears, marmots and people also like these berries. Rabbits and deer eat young raspberry stems.

INTERESTING FACTS

Raspberry is sometimes nick-named "thimble-berry" because the picked berry looks like a thimble.

The stems have lots of prickles! Be careful.

SPECIAL WARNING

21

WILD STRAWBERRY

WHAT IT LOOKS LIKE

Strawberry plants are short. They grow from 3 to 12 inches tall. The stem is hairy.

The leaves grow in threes. They are each about 1 1/2 inches long. They are deep green on top and light green underneath. Both sides can be hairy. The leaf tops have lines running from end to end. The edges have big teeth.

Strawberry flowers are always white. They have 5 petals and a yellow center. They bloom from May to September. The flower is the size of a dime and grows on a stem separate from the leaves.

The single berries are as small as the tip of your finger. Unripe fruit is green. Ripe fruit is bright red. It is shaped like a tiny toy top. It ripens from spring to autumn.

WHERE TO FIND IT

Strawberries grow in sandy soil and lots of sun. Look for them in open fields and along roadsides. They also grow in the edges of open woods and meadows.

Wild strawberries grow from Maine south to Florida, and west to Oklahoma. They also grow from Alaska south to New Mexico.

WHAT EATS IT

This fruit is eaten by quail, grosbeaks, crows, waxwings, robins, deer, chipmunks and squirrels. Rabbits eat the leaves.

INTERESTING FACTS

The name of this fruit may come from a long-ago practice of stringing the berries on straws to sell in the market.

Use a wide bucket for berries so they don't get crushed.

BLUEBERRY

WHAT IT LOOKS LIKE

Short blueberry shrubs grow from 1 to 3 feet tall. The highbush blueberry can grow to 12 feet tall.

The leaves on some kinds of blueberry bushes are dark green with narrow, oval leaves from 1 to 3 inches long. Others are shiny light green, less than 1 inch long, and are very thin.

The flowers are pink-white, and grow in small clusters. They are small and look like bells. Blueberry flowers bloom in May and June.

The fruit is round and the size of a pea. Unripe fruit is green. Ripe fruit is pale blue to blue-black. It ripens in July and August.

WHERE TO FIND IT

Blueberries grow in sandy soil with sunshine. Look in open places like slopes and wood edges.

Different kinds of blueberries grow throughout most of the United States, except in the Desert Southwest.

WHAT EATS IT

Many kinds of wild animals like blueberries: bluebirds, thrushes, kingbirds, grouse, flycatchers, cranes, chipmunks, squirrels, deer, foxes, opossums and bears. People eat blueberries, too.

Wear old clothes. Berry juice can stain.

MAKE SOME BERRY WATER COLORS

You can make watercolor paint with the berries you find (or buy at the store). Make several different kinds so your picture will be more colorful. You can even try mixing two kinds together to make a new color!

WHAT YOU NEED

- Newspaper to protect your work area

- An apron to protect your clothes

- A fine-line black magic marker or pen

- Watercolor art paper

- 1/2 cup of fresh berries, or frozen ones that have been thawed for each color of paint. Softer berries work best (like strawberries, blueberries, or raspberries).

- 1/4 cup of water for each type of berry

- A potato masher or a fork

- A small bowl

- A small strainer

- A clean paintbrush

- A glass with water in it for rinsing the paintbrush

- One small plastic tub for each type of berry used

WHAT TO DO

▼

1. Cover your work area with the newspaper and put on the apron.

2. Using the magic marker or pen, draw a picture on the watercolor art paper. Set it aside to dry.

3. Put 1/2 cup of one type of berries into the bowl and add 1/4 cup water.

4. Mash with the potato masher until everything is *juicy*.

5. Set the strainer across the top of the tub. Strain the juice through it and into the tub. This is the berry watercolor.

6. Repeat the water, mashing and straining steps with the other types of berries.

7. Dip the paintbrush into one of the berry colors and brush it across a part of your picture. (Hint: Watercolors look best when you do not try to stay inside the lines).

8. Then, rinse the paintbrush in the water and try another watercolor.

9. When you are finished painting, let your picture dry.

10. Throw away any extra water colors.

When it is dry, hang your "berry" wonderful picture on the wall!

something to do

SYCAMORE

Interesting Facts

The sycamore is nicknamed "buttonball" for the shape of its spiky fruit.

Long ago, canoes were made from the trunks. One of these was 65 feet long and could carry more than 4 tons!

WHERE TO FIND IT

Sycamores need lots of water. Look for them in the moist soil of woods and fields. Also, in valleys and along wet bottomlands near streams.

WHAT IT LOOKS LIKE

Sycamore trees grow to be about 100 feet tall. The bark is flat and gray. Big patches flake off, leaving behind bare, white spots.

The leaves grow up to 10 inches across. Each leaf has 3 to 5 large dents in the edges. They are shiny green on top, and light green and hairy underneath.

Sycamore seeds make up a hairy, brown, spiky looking fruit that hangs on the tree all winter. It is about the size of a golf ball.

These trees grow across the eastern United States from Maine to Florida, west to Nebraska and into Texas. They also grow in the Southwest.

WHAT EATS IT

Finches and some squirrels eat sycamore fruit. Muskrats and beavers chew the bark and deer eat the twigs.

Take your time and do not hurry.

BEECHNUT

WHAT IT LOOKS LIKE

The beech is a slender tree that can grow over 100 feet tall. The bark is smooth and gray. It may have dark blotches and bands.

The oval leaves are 3 to 5 inches long. They are pointed and tough, with big teeth. The leaves are pale green to blue-green.

The fruit is inside a prickly, four-sided shell about the size of a grape. Two triangle-shaped, shiny brown nuts are inside. When ripe, the four sides of the shell curl up and the nuts drop to the ground.

WHERE TO FIND IT

Beeches sometimes grow by birch and maple trees. Around the base of an old beech tree, the shallow roots may sprout to form a cluster of little trees.

These trees grow throughout the eastern United States, west into Wisconsin and south to Texas.

WHAT EATS IT

Beechnuts are eaten by ruffed grouse, wild turkeys, wood ducks, blue jays, titmice and nuthatches. Raccoons, squirrels, bears and foxes also eat beechnuts.

Interesting Facts

Early settlers stuffed their mattresses with thick beech leaves for softness.

Do not go near any wild animals you might see.

27

PECAN

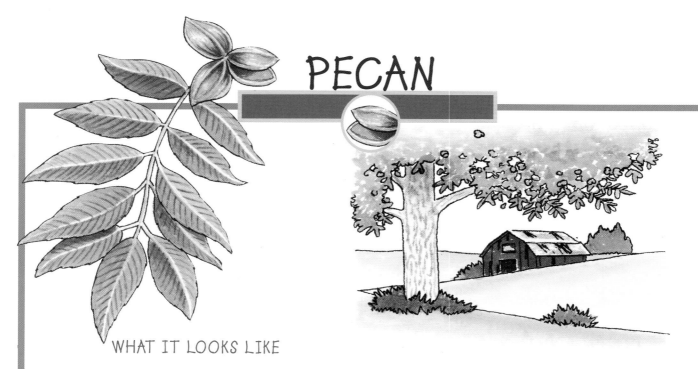

WHAT IT LOOKS LIKE

Pecans are tall, slender trees that grow from 90 to 150 feet tall. The bark is tan-gray with deep ridges.

The leaflets have fine teeth and are about 5 inches long. They are dark yellow-green.

The oval nuts have smooth brown shells and are about 2 inches long. They ripen in September and October in clusters of 3 to 12.

WHERE TO FIND IT

Look for the tree growing in full sun, not in the shade of other trees. It grows in moist areas.

Pecans grow in the South, from near the Atlantic Coast west to Iowa and Texas. Also, from Illinois south to the Gulf of Mexico.

WHAT EATS IT

Squirrels, chipmunks and raccoons eat pecan nuts. Blue jays, woodpeckers and turkeys eat these nuts, too. So do bears and foxes. They are also a favorite food of people.

INTERESTING FACTS

A fully grown pecan tree can produce about a hundred pounds of nuts each year.

Remember to wear sunscreen and insect repellent.

HAWTHORN

WHAT IT LOOKS LIKE

Hawthorn is a shrub. It can grow to be 25 feet tall. The bark is smooth and dark brown. It breaks into thin, scaly plates.

The leaves are 1 to 2 inches long. They are shiny dark green on top, and light green underneath, and hairy. There are not many teeth along the edges. Some kinds of hawthorn have large dents around the edges, others do not.

Hawthorn fruit looks like an apple that is less than 1 inch long. It is orange-red or yellow. There is one nut inside. Short, dry brown curls hang from the bottom of the fruit. The nuts ripen in September.

INTERESTING FACTS

Hawthorn fruit gets its nickname "thornapple" from its shape and thorny branches.

Some Native American tribes believed that eating hawthorn fruit strengthened the heart.

WHERE TO FIND IT

Look in parks and around homes. Hawthorns are planted in these places for their beauty. They are also found along fences and in fields.

In spring, sniff the blossoms. Most hawthorns have an unpleasant smell.

Hawthorns can be found throughout the United States except in the Desert Southwest.

WHAT EATS IT

Hawthorn fruit is a favorite of waxwings, sparrows and grouse. It is also eaten by mice, foxes, rabbits, bears and raccoons. Some people also eat it. Deer eat hawthorn twigs.

SPECIAL WARNING
The sharp thorns of this shrub can grow to be 4 inches long on the branches.

HAZELNUT

This nut is also called a filbert.

Some people believe that holding a hazelnut branch helps them find underground treasures like water or minerals.

WHERE TO FIND IT

Hazelnut shrubs often grow in tangled, overgrown places, like roadsides.

Hazelnuts are ripe in August and September. Look for the shells which are different from other kinds of nuts.

Different types of hazelnuts grow throughout most of the United States.

WHAT IT LOOKS LIKE

The hazelnut is a shrub. It grows from 3 to 8 feet tall. The bark may be light yellow, or brown with tan spots.

There are big teeth along the edges of the rough leaves. The dark green leaves are shaped like hearts. They are 3 to 5 inches long, and woolly underneath.

The dark brown hazelnut is round. Some kinds of hazelnuts grow inside a velvety, green case shaped like a comma. It is about as long as your finger. Other kinds of hazelnuts grow inside a tough, frilly shell in groups of 3 or more. All hazelnuts are about the size of a marble.

WHAT EATS IT

People like hazelnuts. So do squirrels, chipmunks, beavers, rabbits, grouse and woodpeckers.

Take this book with you and have fun!

ACORN

WHAT IT LOOKS LIKE

Acorns grow on oak trees. Oak trees grow to be 20 to 130 feet tall. The bark is gray-brown to dark brown. The bark has deep ridges or is flaky.

Oak leaves are longer than they are wide. They have uneven dents along the edges. White oak leaves have rounded edges without teeth. Black oak leaves have pointed edges and teeth.

Acorns are brown, round nuts inside a cup. They have a smooth, hard shell. Some kinds are as small as grapes, others are as big as golf balls.

WHERE TO FIND IT

Oaks grow in many places, like forests, fields, swamps and in dry places. Oaks also grow around homes and cottages and along roads.

Oak trees grow throughout the United States.

WHAT EATS IT

Acorns are food for wood ducks, ruffed grouse, titmice, deer, mice, bears, squirrels and raccoons.

INTERESTING FACTS

An oak tree can make 1,000 pounds of acorns in a season.

Do not leave behind any litter.

BLACK WALNUT

WHERE TO FIND IT

Look in open woods and valleys along streams. Black walnuts are also found in old fields and pastures. This tree often grows by itself. It likes sunlight.

In autumn, look on the ground for the dark brown shell with the nut inside.

Black walnut trees grow from Massachusetts west to South Dakota and Oklahoma, and south into Florida and west to Texas.

WHAT IT LOOKS LIKE

Black walnut trees grow about 120 feet tall. The bark is dark brown with ridges shaped like diamonds.

The leaflets are yellow-green and up to 5 inches long. They have teeth around the edges.

The nut ripens inside a shell. The shell is covered by a green husk. It is round and about 2 inches across. The husk turns dark brown in autumn.

WHAT EATS IT

Black walnuts are a favorite of many people. Squirrels, bears and raccoons also eat them.

Touching the brown husk will stain your hands and clothes. Wear gloves.

HICKORY

WHAT IT LOOKS LIKE

Hickory trees grow more than 75 feet tall. The bark is gray, and shaggy or scaly.

The leaflets are dark yellow-green with fine teeth on the edges. They are shiny on top. They are about 5 inches long.

The hickory nut grows inside a shell covered by a green-brown husk. It is about 1 inch across and dark brown.

WHERE TO FIND IT

Hickory trees are often found growing next to oak trees. Young hickory trees need shade. The older trees like open, sunny areas.

In autumn, the dark hickory shells split open, and the nut falls out.

Hickories grow from Maine south to Florida and west to Texas and Oklahoma. They also grow from Washington south to California.

WHAT EATS IT

Hickory nuts are liked by grosbeaks, nuthatches, turkeys and woodpeckers. Squirrels, deer, woodchucks and raccoons eat this nut, too. So do people.

INTERESTING FACTS

Some types of hickory bark were used in pioneer days to make green dye.

Do not put your hands into any holes in trees. They may be an animal's home.

MAKE A NUTSHELL BIRD FEEDER

Here's a fun way to use the nuts and seeds you collect,
and give the birds a treat at the same time!

WHAT YOU NEED

- Newspapers to cover your work area
- A spoon
- A small bowl
- Birdfood mixture, made from the recipe below:

  > 1/2 cup peanut butter

  > 2 tablespoons of beef fat or lard

  > 4 tablespoons of seeds gathered from: thistle, dock, dandelion, milkweed, touch-me-not and cattail (or birdseed from a store).

- Empty shells of black walnuts and pecans (You can get these nuts at the store if you want. Break them in half with a nut-cracker. Take out the nuts and mix them into the birdfood.)
- An old board, about 8 to 10 inches long
- Small nails and a small hammer

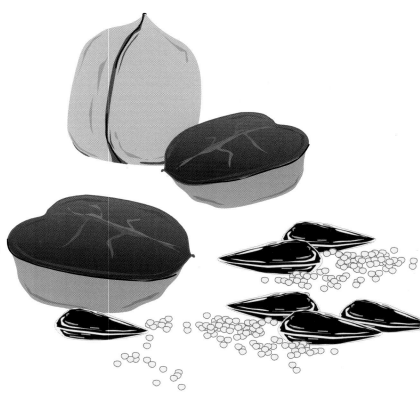

WHAT TO DO

1 Spread the newspapers over your work area.

2 Mix the birdfood ingredients in the bowl using the spoon.

3 Carefully nail the empty walnut and pecan shells to the board using the hammer.

4 Spoon the mixture into the shells and place the board outside on a window ledge or a tree stump.

5 Refill the shells with birdfood when they are empty.

Have fun watching the birds dine at your feeder!

MILKWEED

INTERESTING FACTS

The milkweed's name comes from the milky juice in its stems.

WHAT IT LOOKS LIKE

This plant grows from 1 to 5 feet tall. The stem is thick. Most types have a milky juice inside.

Milkweed leaves are thick and tough. They are smooth and oval and about 6 inches long and 4 inches wide.

The groups of flowers are white, pink or orange. They are smaller than peas and are rubbery. They grow only at the tip of the stem.

The round seeds grow inside seed pods. Each seed is attached to silky threads. The pods are gray-green and have a thick, velvety skin. Some types are bumpy and others are smooth.

WHERE TO FIND IT

Milkweed plants like open spaces and may grow in a patch. Look for them where they will not be crowded by other kinds of plants.

Look for the seed pods in early autumn. They burst open and spill fluffy white parachutes of seeds into the wind.

Milkweed grows almost everywhere across the United States. It grows in woods and swamps, fields and meadows, road-sides and vacant lots.

WHAT EATS IT

Monarch butterflies like milkweed. Goldfinches eat the seeds. Antelopes also eat the plant.

Walk carefully so you do not injure any plants.

DANDELION

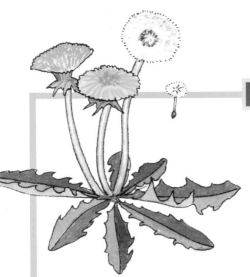

WHAT IT LOOKS LIKE

Dandelions grow between a few inches and 1 1/2 feet tall.

Dandelion leaves are smooth. The edges are deeply cut with triangle shapes. The flower's stem is hollow and has milky juice inside.

Each stem has a yellow flower. The flower has many thin petals and is about the size of a quarter. The flower becomes a ball of white fluff. Each tiny seed is attached to a fluffy thread. The seeds scatter easily when you blow on them.

WHERE TO FIND IT

Look on lawns, fields, roadsides and meadows.

Dandelions grow across the United States, almost anywhere plants are found.

WHAT EATS IT

Bees, and some flies and spiders like the flowers. Goldfinches, siskins, sparrows, grouse and pheasants gobble the seeds. Rabbits, deer, porcupines and gophers like to eat the plants. People sometimes eat young dandelion leaves as salad or dry the root and grind it up to drink like coffee.

The milky juice inside dandelion stems can be harmful if swallowed.

37

WILD ROSE

WHAT IT LOOKS LIKE

Wild rose plants grow from about 1 to 5 feet tall. Some types of rose plants are bushy, others are not.

The oval leaves are as long as your thumb. They are shiny green and have teeth on the edges.

The flowers can be as big as the palm of your hand. They are pink, white, yellow or red. Each flower has a yellow center. Many roses smell good.

Rose seeds are hidden inside a round fruit called a hip that is left over when the flower is gone. It is hard and shiny orange-red. It is about the size of a grape. Several dry, brown curls hang from the bottom. When the rosehip dries up, the seeds fall out.

WHERE TO FIND IT

In summer, the flowers grow along road-sides and fences, and in fields. In autumn, after cold weather comes, look for the bright red hips. They hang like ornaments from the rosebush.

Wild roses grow nearly everywhere in the United States.

WHAT EATS IT

Grouse, thrushes, cedar waxwings, squirrels and mice eat rosehips. Antelope and deer eat the twigs and leaves. Rabbits chew the bark and buds. Some people drink rosehip tea.

INTERESTING FACTS

A long time ago in Europe, hanging a rose over a table meant that all talk beneath it would be kept a secret.

The fruit of the rose is called a "hip." Rosehips have more Vitamin C than oranges.

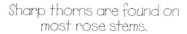

Sharp thorns are found on most rose stems.

SPECIAL WARNING

CATTAIL

WHAT IT LOOKS LIKE

Cattail stems grow up to 6 feet tall. The whole plant is thin. The leaves are less than 3 inches wide. They stick up like ribbons and can grow 3 feet long.

Each plant grows two flower spikes. One is above, and is less noticeable than the bigger spike below it. The bigger one starts out green and turns dark brown. It looks like a large hot dog.

The seeds are cottony yellow inside the brown spikes. In autumn, the spikes burst open and the fluffy seeds blow away.

WHERE TO FIND IT

Look for green cattail shoots in late spring, when they poke out of shallow water. The brown, fuzzy flowers are easily spotted swaying in summer, autumn and winter winds.

Cattails grow throughout the United States in wet places such as ponds, streams, swamps and ditches.

WHAT EATS IT

Geese eat the seeds and roots. Muskrats also eat the roots.

Check to see how deep the water is before you step into it.

39

THISTLE

Some people used to think thistle cured them of sadness. They also thought thistle was a charm against deadly diseases.

WHAT IT LOOKS LIKE

Thistle plants grow from 2 to 5 feet tall. The stems have many branches and can have thorns. Thistle leaves can be thorny, too. They are stiff and narrow. Some have deep cuts on the edges.

The flower is a green ball topped by a rosy-pink, purple or yellow-white tuft. It can be as big as 2 inches across. It blooms in summer.

Thistle seeds form on the flower ball after the petals dry up. The seeds are dark and thin. They ripen in late summer and autumn and are blown away by the wind.

WHERE TO FIND IT

Look for the plant in pastures and along roadsides, especially in sunny places.

Thistle blossoms grow at the very top. Look for the puffy tuft in summer and into September.

Some type of thistle grows almost everywhere in the United States.

WHAT EATS IT

Bees, and painted lady butterflies like the flowers. The seeds are enjoyed by goldfinches, sparrows and chickadees. Antelopes also eat this plant.

Be careful not to hurt yourself on the thistle's sharp spines.

BURDOCK

WHAT IT LOOKS LIKE

Burdock grows from 2 to 8 feet tall. The plant looks bushy. It does not smell good. The stem is dark green and has ridges. The hairy leaves are shaped like hearts and can be as large as dinner plates. They are dull green on top and grayish underneath.

Prickly, rosy-purple flowers bloom in August and September. They are round and about 1 inch across. There are several flowers at the tip of each single red-brown stem. When dry, the prickly flowers become stickers, each about as big as your thumb.

The flat seeds grow from 1 to 2 inches long. They have one ridge. The seeds are dark brown. They grow inside the sticker.

WHERE TO FIND IT

Look in pastures, vacant lots and along roadsides and fences.

Last year s stickers are easy to find on their stalks, at any time of the year.

Burdock grows across the United States.

INTERESTING FACTS

Dried burdock flowers are called "stickers." They hook onto the fur of animals or people's clothing that brush up against them.

An inventor got the idea for Velcro when burdock stickers stuck to his clothes.

WHAT EATS IT

Some people grow burdock as a garden vegetable, and eat the young roots. Pheasants eat the seeds.

Wear gloves to protect your hands.

DOCK

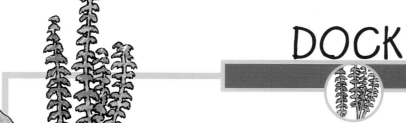

WHAT IT LOOKS LIKE

The plant can grow from 1 to 6 feet tall. It looks ragged and has many branches.

A dock leaf is shaped like a narrow shield. It can be up to 1 foot long. It is green-brown and rough. Some types of dock have leaves with curly edges.

The flowers are bright green and feel scaly.

The seeds are brown and pointed, smaller than popcorn kernels. Each seed has a papery wing around it. The wings are either round or shaped like hearts.

WHERE TO FIND IT

Dock grows almost any-where. Look for it in vacant lots, on roadsides, in marshes and fields. Usually, dock grows in a patch.

Different kinds of dock can be found almost everywhere in the United States.

WHAT EATS IT

Juncos, geese, ducks, rails and bobolinks eat dock seeds. Grouse, pheas-ants and rabbits eat both the leaves and seeds. Deer eat the whole plant.

INTERESTING FACTS

Many years ago in England, people stayed away from dock plants. They thought magicians used the stems to cast spells on people.

Do not hurt any part of a plant with your hands or tools.

42

MAPLE

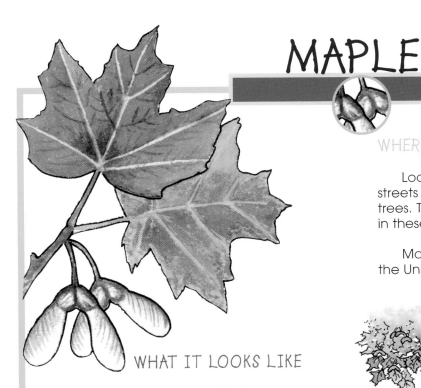

WHERE TO FIND IT

Look in city parks, along streets and in yards for maple trees. They are often planted in these places for shade.

Maple trees grow almost everywhere in the United States.

WHAT IT LOOKS LIKE

Maple trees can grow to be more than 80 feet tall. The bark is silvery and smooth on young trees. It is dark gray-brown with flaky grooves on older trees.

The leaves are shaped like a hand and grow up to 1 foot long and wide.

Maple seeds have wings. Each small seed is closed inside a papery wing. The wing is tan and up to 1 inch long. A pair of seeds are joined at the ends. The joined pair twirls to the ground in autumn.

WHAT EATS IT

Maple seeds are eaten by grosbeaks, grouse and nuthatches. Mice, squirrels and porcupines also eat these seeds. Deer eat the twigs and leaves.

Watch for changes in weather.

43

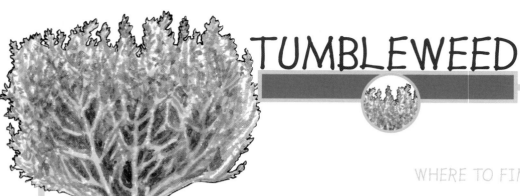

TUMBLEWEED

WHAT IT LOOKS LIKE

Russian thistle is a kind of tumbleweed that grows from 1 to 5 feet tall. It looks like a ball of mostly stems and slender, dark green leaves. The 1/2-inch-long leaves are stiff and have prickles on the tips.

The flowers are small, green-white, or pink-red. They bloom in July.

The seeds grow inside a papery cup. It is small and red and shaped like a toy top.

Late in the growing season, the plant breaks off near the ground. When it is blown by the wind, the seeds scatter to start new plants.

WHERE TO FIND IT

Tumbleweed grows in dry places, like fields and deserts.

The easiest way to find tumbleweed is to look for the dried brown plant ball. It blows across open ground or gets caught against fences.

Tumbleweed can be found in the western and southwestern United States, east to Minnesota and Illinois. It is also found throughout the South, and north to the Mid-Atlantic states.

WHAT EATS IT

Sparrows, pheasants, quail, juncos and larks eat tumbleweed seeds. So do gophers and mice. Antelopes eat the plant. If needed, tumbleweed can be cut green and fed to cattle.

Take drinking water with you.

TOUCH-ME-NOT

WHAT IT LOOKS LIKE

A touch-me-not plant grows from 2 to 5 feet tall. It usually has one thin stem that is light green.

The leaves are pale gray-green. The 3-inch-long leaves are oval with thick teeth on the edges.

Some kinds of touch-me-nots have orange flowers with red spots. Some have solid yellow flowers. Each flower has three petals and is shaped like an open sack. Thin green pods about 1 inch long hold the dark brown seeds. The seeds fall out when the pod dries up.

WHERE TO FIND IT

Touch-me-nots grow in wet, shady places. The plant often looks droopy.

Touch-me-nots grow across most of the eastern United States, south to Alabama and west to Oklahoma.

WHAT EATS IT

Hummingbirds like touch-me-not flowers. The tiny seeds are eaten by quail, mice and squirrels.

INTERESTING FACTS

This plant gets its name because the ripe seed pods burst open when touched.

The juice in the stems can be rubbed on poison ivy rash to help healing.

Touch-me-nots often grow near poison ivy. Watch out!

PLANT A SEED GARDEN

You can plant a seed garden in spring if you have gathered seeds the year before. Or you can plant in autumn right after a seed-gathering trip. If you do not want to plant your seeds in the ground, you can put soil in a large pot or bucket that has a hole in the bottom. Plant your seeds and put the pot in a sunny spot outside—in the yard, or on a patio or balcony.

WHAT YOU NEED

- A sunny, unused corner of your yard.

- A spade or shovel

- A rake

- A watering can, or a hose for water

- Collected seeds from sun-loving plants such as thistle, dandelion, milkweed, dock and wild rose. If you have a shady place, try touch-me-nots, too.

WHAT TO DO

▼

1. Be sure to get permission before you dig up a corner of your yard.

2. Use the spade to dig up the chosen area.

3. Remove all clumps of grass, and any rocks.

4. Rake the area smooth.

5. Sprinkle the seeds across the raked area.

6. Cover the seeds very lightly with some soil.

7. Water gently. Water again during dry times.

8. Be patient. The seeds may need a winter's rest before they sprout.

You will never have to weed your seed garden. Any weeds that show up will likely be welcomed as additional food by the birds and other animals!

SCRAPBOOK

Berries, Nuts and Seeds

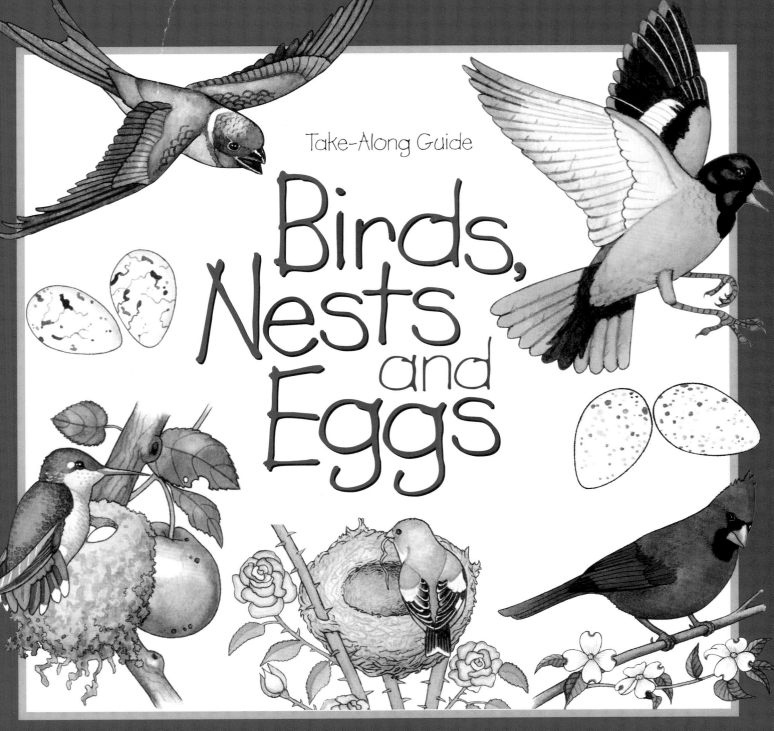

Take-Along Guide

Birds, Nests and Eggs

by Mel Boring

illustrations by Linda Garrow

INTRODUCTION

What makes birds different from other animals is their WINGS. With those powerful wings, they escape enemies, find new supplies of food, and migrate to warmer places so they can survive winter.

Hundreds of years ago, people knew very little about birds. Some even thought birds went to the moon when they migrated. Now we know more about birds, but there is still much to learn, and a lot to enjoy.

The best time to watch birds is when they are most active: between 6 o'clock and 10 o'clock in the morning. In fact, for people who really like to watch birds, there is a bird-counting program called "Project Feeder-Watch." For more information, you can write to:

Coordinator
Project FeederWatch—Cornell University
159 Sapsucker Woods Road
Ithaca, New York 14850

Most birds don't use their nests more than one season. However, birds like robins do return to the same neighborhood every year. One good way to find most bird nests is to watch for birds carrying nest-building materials in their beaks. You will see this most often in spring or early summer. Then follow the bird quietly to its nest.

It's okay to take a close look at a bird's nest. Most birds are not easily disturbed. But DON'T TOUCH the nest or eggs or babies. And, of course, if the birds put up a fuss, leave the nest right away.

This Take-Along Guide and its activities will help you know some of the wonderful birds you can find. You can use the ruler on the back of this book to figure out how big the birds would be up close. You can bring a pencil and use the Scrapbook to draw what you see.

Discover and have fun in the world of Birds, Nests and Eggs!

AMERICAN ROBIN

Bird

The robin's happy "*Cheer-up!*" seems to sing away winter and bring on spring. You will see the robin on the lawn tugging up earthworms.

Robins also eat caterpillars, beetles, crickets and spiders—and fruits like apples, cherries and raspberries.

With its red-orange chest, the American robin is the bird we know best. The robin is 9 to 11 inches long. Male robins have dark heads. Female robins have dull gray heads and tails, and grayish legs. Young robins have spots on their undersides.

When temperatures reach above 37°F watch for your first robin. This usually happens beginning in March to early April.

Robins migrate south to warmer weather in the fall. In the winter, they gather in huge groups along the Gulf of Mexico.

Nest

Female robins build the nests, but the male sometimes brings her building materials. She weaves a circle of grasses, twigs, scraps of rags and string. Inside the nest, she molds a cup of mud to fit her body. Look for their first nest in April, and the second as late as August.

A robin's first nest will probably be in a pine, cedar, or spruce tree. Look for their second nest in broadleaf trees, like an elm, maple, oak, willow, poplar or apple. They build their nests between 5 and 70 feet from the ground.

You can help a robin build its nest. Dig up some clay-like wet mud and put it in a pan near the trees in your yard.

Eggs

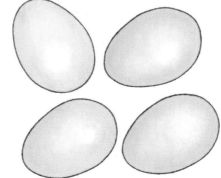

The robin usually lays 4 eggs. They are green-blue, and each would fit on a quarter. The female sits on them for 12 to 14 days. About 9 to 12 days after hatching, the young birds start to fly.

SOMETHING INTERESTING
ABOUT
American Robins

One robin can eat as much as 14 feet of earth-worms in one day.

55

HOUSE SPARROW

House sparrows are very messy birds. And sometimes they chase away other birds like woodpeckers and swallows.

With its chestnut-colored hat and black bib around its neck, the male house sparrow looks dressed up for dinner. Females don't look so dressed up. They are colored streaky brown and dingy white. House sparrows are 5 to 6 inches long.

Though it is a songbird, the house sparrow doesn't have much of a song. It makes a shrill, noisy "*cheep*" and "*chissick.*"

Bird

Just 150 years ago there were no house sparrows in the United States. Then in 1850, 16 of them were brought to New York City from England. Today there are over 150 million house sparrows in North America. It is one of the most common birds in the world.

SOMETHING INTERESTING
ABOUT
House Sparrows

It will fill its white cheeks with almost anything: seeds, grains, insects, fruits, flowers and scraps.

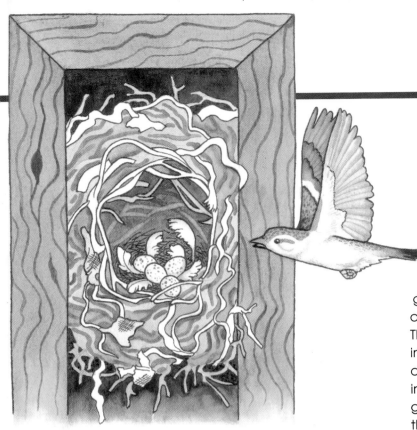

Nest

A house sparrow's nest looks like a big mess. The male and female build it of grass, weeds, twigs, feathers, string, paper and trash. It is round and has a side door. The sparrows stuff the nest into any hole inside or outside of buildings or in birdhouses at least 5 feet off the ground. Or it might be in a tree, as high as 60 feet from the ground. Look for the nest from February through July.

Eggs

Sparrows lay 5 or 6 whitish eggs with brown speckles. Each egg is a little bigger than a quarter. The female sits on the eggs for 9 to 18 days. The young birds can fly 11 to 18 days after hatching.

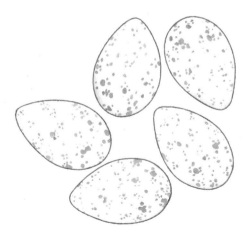

NORTHERN CARDINAL

Bird

The cardinal is the state bird of more states than any other, and is probably our most popular bird. Male cardinals are easy to spot. They are our only all-red birds with red crests on their heads. They have a black mask across their eyes and under their red-orange beaks. Cardinals are about 8 inches long.

The female cardinal is mostly rosy-yellow, with a few touches of red. Up close, her beak looks as if she is wearing orangeish lipstick.

It is easy to get cardinals to come to feeders because they eat over 100 different kinds of food. Their favorite is sunflower seeds. They also like cracked corn, millet and even peanut butter!

Cardinals sing beautiful songs. You may hear a "*Hip-hooray!*" or "*birdy-birdy-birdy!*" Cardinals can sing 28 different songs.

SOMETHING INTERESTING ABOUT Northern Cardinals

Each year cardinals can be found farther north. Now the cardinal has even reached Canada.

Nest

Cardinals begin nesting earlier than most birds. Starting in late March or early April, they might raise 4 broods by the end of summer. The nest is a deep cup of twigs, roots, bark and leaves, lined with grass or animal hair. It is usually hidden in thick shrubs, 2 to 10 feet from the ground.

To figure out where the cardinals are nesting, watch for them both flying into a thicket with nest materials. Or listen for the female singing from the nest. Also, follow the male when he flies to the bush with food in his beak for her.

Eggs

A cardinal egg is about as big as a quarter. It is bluish-white, with reddish-brown spots. The female sits on the 3 or 4 eggs for 12 or 13 days. Young cardinals can fly 10 days after hatching.

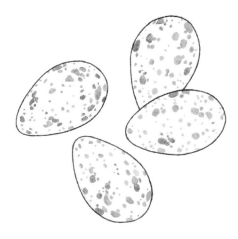

BLUE JAY

Bird

Loud calls of "*Jay! Jay!*" come from a bird feeder. You know it's a blue jay even before you see it. The other birds all fly away at the blue jay's danger signal—and the clever jay gobbles up all of the sunflower seeds!

With a blue crest and back, bright blue-white-black wings and tail, a blue jay looks as if it has on a blue coat and white underwear. Males and females are colored the same. Jays can grow up to 1 foot long.

The big blue jay hangs around thick shrubs and trees—especially oak—all year long.

Blue jays depend on acorns for food, which they bury for winter. They also like bread, corn and peanuts. Sometimes they eat insects, frogs, salamanders and even mice.

SOMETHING INTERESTING ABOUT Blue Jays

The blue jay is a strong flier. It is able to carry four acorns at a time in its throat and beak. It can easily fly five miles with this load.

Nest

Though blue jays hang around oaks, their favorite place to nest is in a pine tree, starting in April. They hide their nest in the crotch of the tree. The jay's nest is shaggy-looking—made of sticks and lined with grass and their feathers. Their nest could be anywhere from 5 to 50 feet off the ground.

A male blue jay tries to trick people and other animals from finding its nest by landing at the base of a tree and hopping around and around on the trunk, as if going up a "spiral stairway."

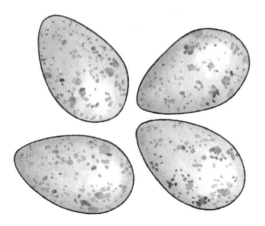

Eggs

Blue jay eggs are green with brown spots. Usually there are 4 or 5 eggs, each a little bigger than a quarter. Both the male and female incubate the eggs, which take about 17 days to hatch. In 17 more days, the young jays start to fly.

NORTHERN ORIOLE

Bird

Northern orioles arrive late in April with a burst of sound and color. Males perch on high places and sing out clear little songs. One is "*Hew-LEE!*"

The male oriole is bright orange on its chest, and black on top, with touches of white on the wings and a black head. Females are olive-brown with duller orange. Orioles are about 8 inches long.

You will find northern orioles around tall shade trees like elms and maples. And once they have paired up, the male and female keep in touch by singing almost all the time.

To get a closer look at orioles, you can use an orange to attract them. Pound a nail halfway into a tree and stick an orange half on it—fruit side out. It usually takes only a few hours for them to find it.

Nest

The northern oriole's nest is usually in a tall shade or fruit tree. It looks like a pouch with a top-hole, hung from the end of a drooping branch. The female weaves the nest together using plant stems, then lines it with fine grass and feathers. It hangs between 6 and 60 feet from the ground.

In their hanging nest, northern oriole babies may be rocked to sleep by the wind. The nest is very strong, however, and often stays in place all through the harsh winter.

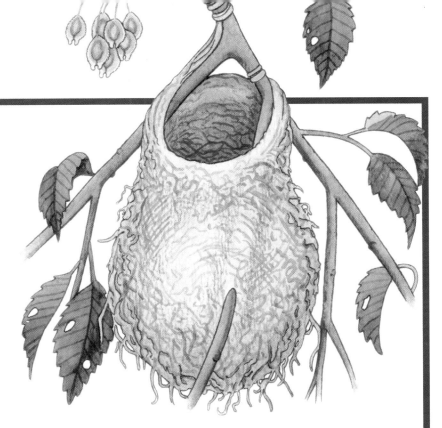

Eggs

One oriole egg is laid each day for 4 to 6 days. The eggs are a bit bigger than nickels. They are gray-white with brown and black blotches. The female sits on the eggs for about 12 to 14 days. Two weeks later the young orioles start to fly.

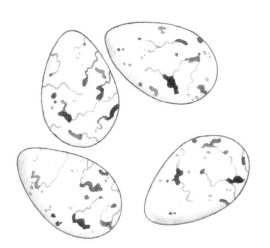

MAKE A "BLIND" FOR BIRD WATCHING

Birds fly away whenever you go near them. It isn't your scent or bright clothing that frightens them most. It is your movement. Here is how you can get right up next to the birds: Make a tent out of an old sheet or blanket that you can make holes in, or use a big appliance box to hide you from the birds while you are bird watching.

WHAT YOU NEED

- An old sheet or blanket that you have permission to use and cut holes in.

–OR–

- A large appliance box, like the one a stove, refrigerator or air conditioner comes in. But any big box will work, if it will hold two people your size—for you and a friend.

WHAT TO DO

1 Decide where you want to put your "hide." Make sure it will be near where birds usually eat on the grass or at a feeder.

2 Set up a "blind" by draping the sheet or blanket over lawn chairs, picnic table or clothes line. Put rocks on the ends of the material to keep it from blowing around.—OR— Set up the box in an open place on the grass.

3 Cut a watch-hole in the widest side, about 6 inches from the top, in the center. Make the hole 2 inches high and 6 inches wide, big enough for you to look through.

4 Cut a doorway on the side opposite the watch-hole. Make it big enough for you to crawl through, about 18 inches high and 18 inches wide. Cut it near the center.

5 Don't go near the "blind" for several days. Birds will stay away at first. But when they see that it isn't going to move, they will become used to it, and eat as usual.

6 Then you can creep into your "hide" and wait patiently for the birds to come. Early morning or early afternoon is best. Remember to sit still.

SPECIAL TIPS

Bring binoculars for a closer view of the birds.

Take along a flashlight and this book to read while you wait.

Use the scrapbook pages to write down what you see.

You can even bring along a quiet snack to eat. Raisins and grapes are good treats, but not a crisp, crunchy apple—or crackly potato chips!

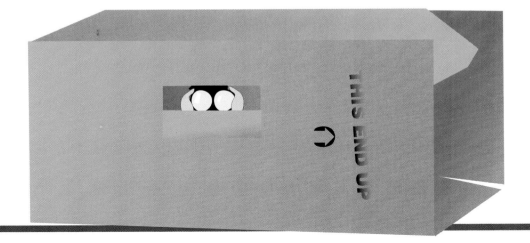

RUBY-THROATED HUMMINGBIRD

Bird

The hummingbird weighs no more than a penny. It is only about 3-1/2 inches long and bathes on a flower leaf with dewdrop water.

Yet, this tiny flying jewel can attack other much bigger birds flying too close to its nest—and win the battle. It can out-fly any bird and fly in any direction, even backward and upside-down at the same time. And hummingbirds are fast fliers. Their average speed is 30 mph, but they have been clocked up to 50 mph.

Ruby-throated hummingbirds have shiny green heads, backs and tails, and gray-white chests. Only the male has the brilliant, glittering, ruby-red throat that gives this humming-bird its name.

Look for hummers beginning in May, when their favorite flowers start to bloom. They sip nectar and snack on small insects around them. They like red flowers best. Especially tube-shape flowers like honeysuckle, morning glory, petunias and lilacs.

Nest

A hummingbird nest is the size of half a golf ball. It is placed near the fork of a tree branch. Look for the nests in apple, maple, oak or pine trees.

Nests are built in May or June, perhaps as high up as 60 feet. The female hummingbird builds it with plant fuzz, lichens and bark. The whole thing is held together with spider web.

Eggs

Hummingbirds lay only 2 eggs. They are white and smaller than a dime. Females sit on them for 14 to 16 days. The tiny birds begin to fly between 22 and 24 days after hatching.

AMERICAN GOLDFINCH

Bird

Goldfinches seem to be happy birds, and their songs tell it. You will hear them in April and May, calling out "*potato-chips.*" But they don't eat potato chips, they really like thistle seeds. Goldfinches will stay around all summer if there are thistle seeds in a bird feeder—maybe even all winter.

Goldfinches swoop up and down as if on a roller coaster when they fly. They spend lots of time in flocks through June. They frolic about, singing, then eating, then singing and eating again, nonstop.

American goldfinches eat mostly seeds and a few insects. They are about as long as your hand and grow to be about 5 inches long.

The male is golden yellow, with a black cap tipped over his eyes, and black wings with white bars on them. In winter, he loses some of his bright coloring and looks the same as the female. She is mostly olive-yellow, with no black cap, less black on her wings and a whitish chest. By May, males turn gold again.

The nest is woven together so tightly that it would even hold water.

Nest

Goldfinches nest late in summer—July and August—in upright forks of bushes or small trees about 4 to 14 feet off the ground. They especially like to nest in apple, elm, maple, cottonwood, willow or pine trees, and roses or thistles.

The female builds the nest of fine grasses, bark and moss. Then it is lined with thistledown and silk from caterpillars.

Eggs

Goldfinches lay 4 to 6 blue-white eggs, smaller than pennies. The male brings the female food while she sits on the eggs. The eggs hatch in 12 to 14 days, and the babies can fly two weeks later. The young birds eat seeds already chewed by their parents.

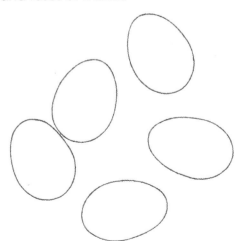

RED-WINGED BLACKBIRD

Bird

The male red-winged blackbird looks like an army general. With red and yellow shoulder patches the black bird seems to screech out orders: "*Oaka-LEE!*" His calls are squeaky sing-songs.

The female looks dressed like a soldier, in dull browns and white on her wings and chest. She speaks with shorter, softer whistles, "*Tee-tee-tee-tee-tee.*" Red-winged blackbirds grow to be 7 to 9 inches long.

Redwings usually settle in marshy spots and they eat weed and marsh plant seeds, insects and fruit. They might even visit your feeder as early as March.

SOMETHING INTERESTING

ABOUT

Red-Winged Blackbirds

They gather in flocks to migrate south for winter. Blackbird flocks are famous. One bird watcher saw a flock of 30,000 black-birds flying.

Nest

Red-winged blackbirds build nests around cattail stalks from late April to early July. The female may use swamp milkweed strips wound around the stalks to make a cradle to hang her nest in. Into this she presses a deep cup of coarse grasses, lined with fine grass.

If you are near a redwing's nest, both male and female will cry out, "*Check!*" or "*Tseeert!*"—their danger calls. Also, the female will fly straight up from the nest when startled.

Red-winged blackbird nests are also found in trees or thickets. These may be near the ground, or as high as 20 feet up in the tree.

Eggs

The eggs are blue-green, with streaks, blotches and spots of purple, black or brown. The spots wash off if the eggs get wet. Only the female incubates the eggs. The 3 to 5 quarter-size eggs hatch in 11 days—and 11 days later the new redwings can fly.

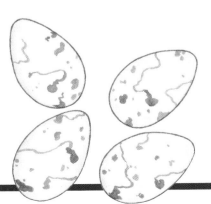

BARN SWALLOW

Bird

Barn swallows make flying look easy. They can even eat while flying. They fly low over water and splash into it when they want a quick bath.

Both male and female barn swallows are red, white and blue. Their face is reddish, a white band circles the back of their neck and their heads and backs are blue. Their belly is rusty-colored. A third of their body length is tail, with a wide fork at the end. They are about 6 to 7 inches long.

Barn swallows make a musical twitter most of the time. It sounds like they are chattering to music: "*tswit-tswit, tswit-tswit.*" Listen and watch for them to come swooping and looping your way late in April or early May. In September they will dash and dart away.

Nest

Barn swallows make their nests almost entirely of mud. They stick them to ledges outside or inside buildings from May to July using more mud. It is plastered in small dabs with straw between layers. The nest is lined with grass and feathers, and is only as big as half a teacup. It may be just above your head, or up to 20 feet from the ground.

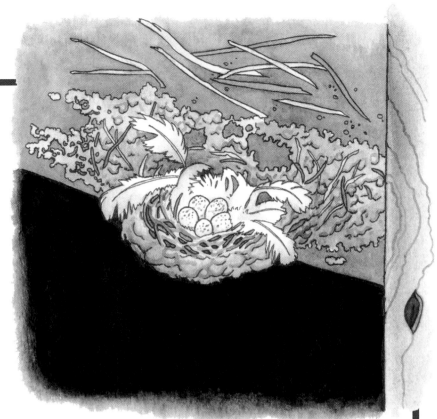

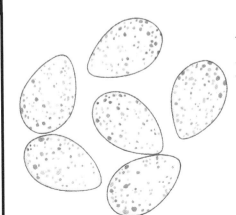

Eggs

Barn swallows lay 3 to 6 penny-size eggs. They are white with brown spots. Both parents sit on the eggs for about 2 weeks. They take turns bringing food to the babies until they can fly at 3 weeks old.

Barn swallows, like most birds, have a "hatching patch" on their tummy, a bare, warmer spot for the eggs.

GIVE THE BIRDS A SHOWER-BATH

Birds need water to drink—and to play in! Some birds love to run through a lawn sprinkler, or even a drippy water faucet. Here's a way to give them some water fun, and you a lot of bird watching fun.

WHAT YOU NEED

- An old pail with a small leak, or punch a small hole in the bottom.

- An old pie pan or plastic pail lid that is shallow, no deeper than 1 or 2 inches. Or use an old garbage-can lid.

WHAT TO DO

1 Hang the pail from a tree limb that is low enough for you to reach.

2 Underneath it, place the pan or lid.

3 Fill the hanging pail with water so that it drips water in the pool underneath.

Now stand back and bird watch. You may be surprised to see how *many* different kinds of birds will come running—and flying—for a shower-bath. After all, birds like to keep cool on a hot day too!

SPECIAL TIPS

If you don't have an old bucket, try hanging a garden hose on the tree limb over the pan.

Turn the water on so it just trickles, and makes a little splash.

BLACK-CAPPED CHICKADEE

Bird

A chickadee is sitting on a branch when a bug flies by. The bird drops off backward, catches the bug in mid-air, does a somersault, and lands on its feet. Chickadees are bird-world acrobats!

The chickadee has a tiny beak made for digging into cracks for bug eggs no bigger than pinheads. They also like sunflower seeds, suet and finely cracked corn.

A black-capped chickadee weighs no more than four pennies. They have black caps and black bibs, with white faces and chests. Males and females look the same, and are about 5 inches long. You can hear them calling "*CHICKA-dee-dee-dee!*" all year long.

Little chickadees stay warm in winter because they have downy feathers right next to their skin—like thermal underwear. Their outer feathers are like a winter overcoat. Chickadees flit around even on below-zero winter days.

SOMETHING INTERESTING ABOUT Black-Capped Chickadees

Chickadees are such good bug-finders that other birds, like nuthatches and woodpeckers, follow them to find bugs.

Nest

The chickadee's nest is usually in a rotted tree branch or stump, from 4 to 15 feet up—sometimes as high as 50 feet. April to June, the male and female dig out a nest by carrying away the rotted wood, beakful by beakful. They line the hollow with moss, plant down, hair, fur and wool.

The best way to find a chickadee nest (April through June) is to watch for two chickadees that perch and drop wood chips from their bills.

Eggs

Chickadees lay from 5 to 8 penny-size eggs. They are white and speckled with red-brown. The female sits on them for about 12 days and the babies leave the nest 2 weeks later.

DOWNY WOODPECKER

Bird

The downy woodpecker has been called "a friendly jackhammer." It is the smallest and tamest of the woodpeckers. If you walk up to a tree trunk it is on, it usually won't fly away. It scoots up behind the tree, and maybe it will peek around the tree at you. Downies make a light "*keek keek*" sound, and another sound like the whinny of a tiny horse.

The downy woodpecker's beak is like a chisel, flat and sharp, not pointed like most bird beaks. Downies find food by tapping the tree. The woodpecker hears bugs moving inside the tree and chisels them out.

The downy is black and white, with a white stripe down its back, and white stripes on its wings. Males have a patch of red on the back of their heads.

Downy woodpeckers nest in the holes of trees old enough to have large dead limbs, in April or May. To find one, listen for continual hammering, rather than short tapping that other birds make. Also look for wood chips at the base of the tree.

After the babies are a few days old, downy woodpecker parents have to feed them as often as once every minute!

Nest

The entrance to the downy's hole is as big as a half-dollar, and opens into a hollow inside. The hollow is about as big as a football. There is no nest, except a few wood chips. Downy nests are built between 5 and 40 feet above the ground.

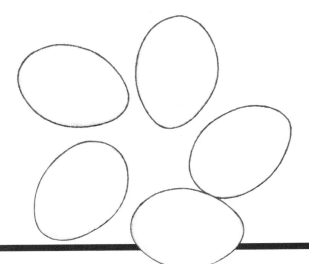

Eggs

Downy woodpecker eggs are about penny-size. Usually there are 4 or 5, and they are pure white. Both parents incubate the eggs equally, for about 12 days. In about 3 weeks, the new woodpeckers start to fly.

WHITE-BREASTED NUTHATCH

Bird

The nuthatch could be called an upside-down bird. It zigzags down a tree trunk head-first. It stops, points its head straight out from the tree, and calls "*Yank, yank!*" It sounds like a little toy horn.

The little white-breasted nuthatch is blue-gray, with a turned up bill. The male's cap is jet-black; the female's is lighter and more silvery. That is the only color difference between them. Nuthatches are 5 to 6 inches long.

As it hops down the bark, it nips and nabs beetles, ants and other insects and their eggs, as well as caterpillars, spiders and flies. It also eats acorns, hickory nuts and beechnuts.

The nuthatch stashes parts of the bugs it finds under bark. They are saved for later—maybe winter—in its "bark bank."

Nest

Nuthatches make nests in knot holes with wood rotted out behind them, in April to June. The male carries bark, twigs, grass, feathers and hair to the door. The female makes the nest. She stacks up bark, then weaves the other materials into a "mattress."

You will usually find the white-breasted nuthatch's nest in a big shade tree, from 5 to 50 feet off the ground.

Eggs

Nuthatch eggs are white and speckled with brown. They are a little bigger than pennies. There are 4 to 10 eggs per nest. The female sits on the eggs constantly, seldom flying out, even to eat. They hatch in 12 days. In 2 weeks, the newborns learn to climb down the tree like their parents, head-first. Then they learn to fly.

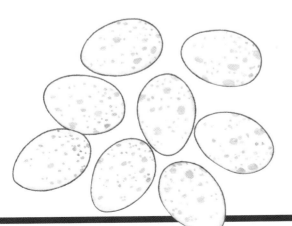

MAKE A HANG-DOWN SUET FEEDER

Many birds seldom feed at regular feeders.
But they love beef suet, and using a net bag—the kind that fruit and
vegetables sometimes come in—you can give them a treat.

WHAT YOU NEED

- Suet. It is a solid white beef fat. If you ask at a meat counter and tell them you want it to feed the birds, they might even give it to you for free. It comes in smaller or bigger chunks—either is okay.

- A net bag. It is the kind that onions, potatoes, and sometimes apples and oranges come in.

- About 2 feet of string.

WHAT TO DO

1 Put 3 small pieces and 3 big pieces of suet in the net bag.

2 Bunch the bag's top together and tie one end of the string tightly around it.

3 Tie the other end of the string around a tree branch or railing that is strong enough to hold the bag.

SPECIAL TIP

If your bag already has pull-handles, pull them tight and tie one end of the string through the loops.

OTHER THINGS TO DO

Roll the suet in different kinds of birdseed. See which kinds the birds like best.

You can use different colored bags.

Make notes in the back of this book about which birds come to the feeder, and what seeds and color of bags they like best— or don't like.

The suet feeder works best in winter, when the birds can't find much food outdoors. If you hang the suet bag up in the summer, be sure to refill it with fresh suet about once a week, so it doesn't spoil before the birds eat it all up.

MEADOWLARK

Bird

When a meadowlark crouches quietly in weeds that match its back feathers, it seems to vanish. When it stands up and puffs out its chest, it looks like a yellow flag. Its upper parts are brown-streaked and it has a brilliant yellow chest with a black V on it. Male and female mead-owlarks look alike, but the female's colors are a little duller. Meadowlarks are between 8 and 11 inches long.

The Eastern meadowlark sings a high, slurry "*See-you, see-yeeeer.*" The Western meadowlark sings out a lower, louder, longer, more flute-like song.

Meadowlarks have beaks that are long and strong. Meadowlarks use their beaks to poke into bug holes for dinner. They live in grassland and only eat seeds in the harsh winter.

You will hear the mead-owlark when it arrives in late March or early April, singing from fence posts.

Nest

A meadowlark nest is hard to find. But these birds are fun and easy to watch if you do find a nest, because it is on the ground. The female builds it of grasses and weeds. She hides it by building a grass dome over the top and never flies down to it. She tunnels under the weeds to get to it. If you get too close, she will call out a warning "*Dzert!*"

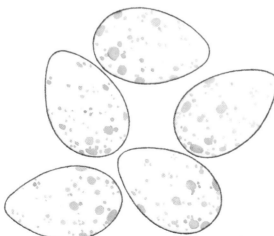

Eggs

There are usually 5 meadowlark eggs, white with brown or purple spots—a little smaller than a half-dollar. The female sits on them for about two weeks. In 11 to 12 days, the meadowlark babies can fly.

MOURNING DOVE

They put very little lining in the nest. It is so thin that eggs can be seen through the twigs from below.

Bird

The mourning dove is a gentle, peaceful bird. It calls "*Ooah, cooo, cooo, coo.*" You can also hear the whistling of its wings as it flies.

Mourning doves eat seeds, especially corn and sunflower seeds. They have long, pointy tails and small round heads. They are gray on top and the color of a fawn beneath—their soft colors seem to glow. Mourning doves are about 12 inches long. Males and females look alike, though the female is a little smaller, and duller in color.

The best time to see mourning doves is April to July mornings when they are nesting. Look for doves carrying twigs in their beaks.

Nest

The mourning dove nest is a loose jumble of sticks laid on a branch in low bushes or a tall tree. Their nest is on the ground sometimes. Most often they build it between 3 and 30 feet off the ground. Both male and female build it, between late May and late July.

Though mourning doves prefer nesting in evergreens, look for them also in apple, elm, maple, oak and willow trees.

Eggs

Mourning doves usually lay 2 white eggs, each a little bigger than a quarter. The parents spend equal time incubating them for 2 weeks.

The young doves are fed "pigeon milk." It is a white, cheesy liquid made in the parents' stomachs from seeds they eat. It's pumped from their stomachs to their beaks and into the babies' bills. The babies can fly in 2 weeks.

KILLDEER

Bird

This bird won't let you forget its name. It shouts it at you: "*Killdeer!*" The killdeer is one of the world's noisiest birds.

Besides its call, the best way to recognize a killdeer is by the black double necklace around its neck. It is dark brown on top and white on the bottom. It eats earthworms and insects. Males and females look alike, and are between 9 and 11 inches long.

The killdeer is famous for its "broken-wing" trick. If you come near its nest, it hobbles away with wings dragging, crying as if its wing is broken. A killdeer does this to draw you away from the nest. When you leave, the clever bird returns to its nest.

Killdeers migrate in October, and are some of the earliest birds to come back in March.

Nest

Killdeers are very sneaky nesters. Their nest is hardly even a nest. It is just a shallow hollow on the ground with stones and a little grass around it.

To find the killdeer's nest, put a marker where you first saw the bird and walk in a spiral around the marker, each circle a little farther from it. Watch carefully up to 100 feet from the marker—you should eventually find it.

Eggs

Killdeer eggs are as big as silver dollars. Most often there are 4 of them, light brown with darker splotches. The male and female take turns sitting on them for 24 to 28 days. Baby killdeers leave the nest as soon as their feathers are dry.

SCRAPBOOK
Birds, Nests and Eggs

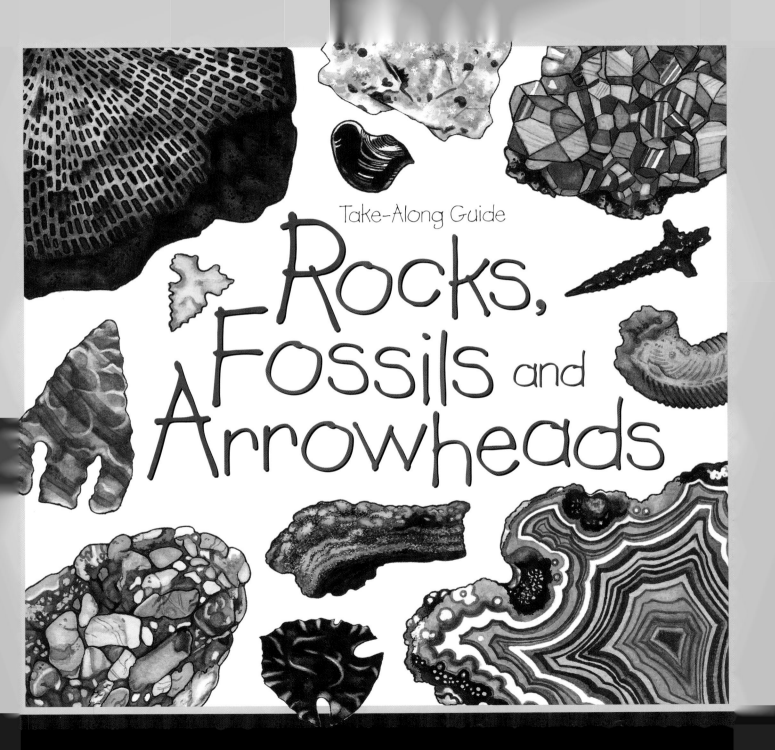

Take-Along Guide

Rocks,
Fossils and
Arrowheads

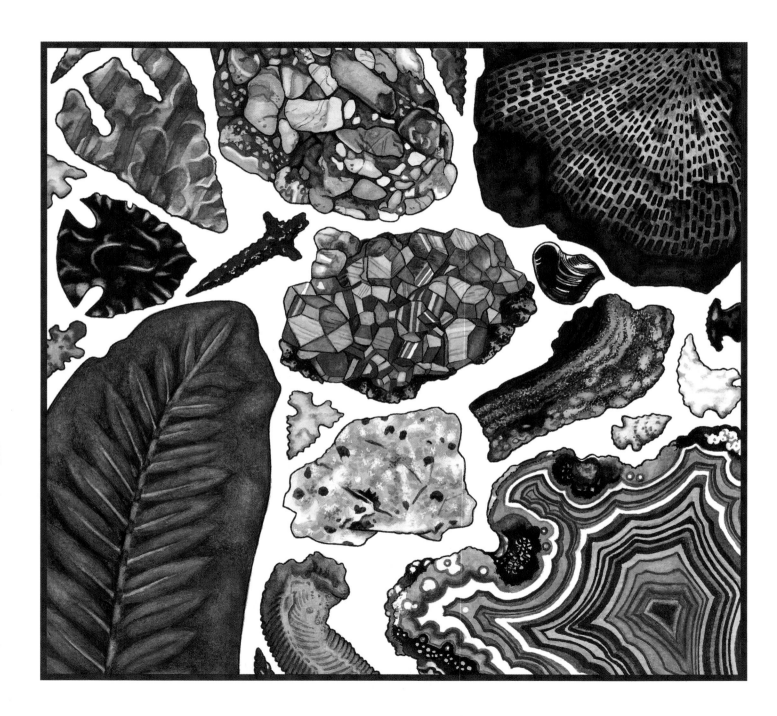

INTRODUCTION

Collecting rocks, minerals, fossils, arrowheads, and other artifacts can be lots of fun! By learning more about them, you will learn about the history of the earth.

Scientists believe that Earth is over 4.5 billion years old. It is made up of many kinds of minerals, which bind together to form rocks. Depending on which minerals combine and how they are pressed together, they form different kinds of rocks.

Both minerals and rocks come in many different colors and combinations of colors. They may be very hard, or they may be soft or flaky. Some rocks are very smooth, and others are bumpy.

Sometimes, as rocks were forming, plants and animals were trapped inside them. Sometimes their body parts were replaced by other minerals, and then turned to stone. They are called fossils. And they help scientists determine the age of the rock.

Arrowheads and other artifacts were made and used by Native Americans. Heavy rocks were used as tools for grinding and crushing. Softer rocks that were easy to chip into sharp points were used for knives and weapons. Scientists study them to learn about how these people lived.

This Take-Along Guide and its activities will help you find, identify, and learn about the specimens, or samples, you see. You can use the ruler on the back cover to measure what you find. You can bring along a pen or pencil and draw what you see in the Scrapbook.

Have fun exploring the world of Rocks, Fossils and Arrowheads!

ROCKS & MINERALS

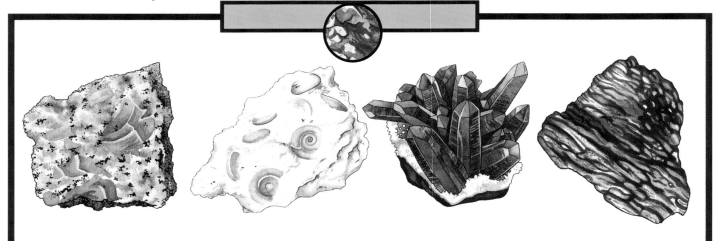

Most rocks are made up of at least two minerals. In addition to making up rocks, individual minerals can form into shapes called crystals. Some crystals are very large and you can easily see them on the surface of the rock. Sometimes the crystals are too small to see without a microscope.

Geologists who study rocks classify them according to how the rocks were formed. The three main types of rock are igneous, sedimentary, and metamorphic.

Hot, liquid magma is found deep in the earth. When it comes to the surface, it is called lava and often flows out of volcanoes. The minerals in magma may cool slowly or quickly. Rocks made in the cooled and hardened magma are called igneous rocks.

Some rocks are formed in water environments. These rocks are often layer upon layer of shells and marine animals that have been compressed together. Or they are pieces of gravel cemented together by sand particles. They are called sedimentary rocks.

Sometimes, deep in the earth, one kind of rock is under such great heat and pressure that it changes into another kind of rock. It may have started out as an igneous or a sedimentary rock. They may look as if they have been squeezed or folded over. These are called metamorphic rocks.

BASALT

WHAT IT LOOKS LIKE

The most common rock on Earth is basalt. It makes up about 70 percent of the Earth's surface. And most of the ocean floor is basalt.

This igneous rock is usually black or very dark gray in color. It is very fine grained, and sometimes you can see dark green crystals.

WHERE TO FIND IT

In wet climates, weathering sometimes turns basalt to clay. In Hawaii, the black sand beaches are made of weathered basalt.

The first lava to come out of a volcano is usually basalt. And it can quickly flow for hundreds of miles, forming thick sheets over the ground.

Basalt is also found where shifting continental plates have pulled and stretched the earth, such as in California, Oregon, Washington, and New Mexico.

Devil's Tower in Wyoming is a very large formation of basalt.

WHAT IT'S USED FOR

Where roads have been cut through areas of basalt, the walls look like big, dark building blocks stacked on top of each other.

Basalt that has been sandwiched between layers of sandstone is called "traprock." This makes a strong rock, and it is often crushed and used for building materials.

Take drinking water with you when you go exploring.

GRANITE

WHAT IT LOOKS LIKE

This igneous rock is usually light in color, with a combination of white, gray, pink, yellow, tan, and possibly flecks of black minerals.

It is coarse-grained, and because the minerals in granite cooled slowly in the magma, larger crystals are visible.

WHERE TO FIND IT

It is usually present where continental plates collided. That is, at the core of old mountains that were formed by the earth folding.

One large outcropping of granite is Yosemite National Park's Half Dome. Because this rock resists weathering, large geological features are usually made of granite. Well-known examples in the United States are Stone Mountain in Georgia and Mount Rushmore in South Dakota.

WHAT IT'S USED FOR

Some gravel is made of granite. Depending on the mineral content, powdered granite can be used as fertilizer.

Slabs of granite can be shined to a smooth finish for tabletops, counters, and floor tiles. Granite may also be used for decorative stone pieces found in buildings.

Monuments, paving blocks, and cemetery markers are often made of granite.

INTERESTING FACTS

A piece of granite that measures about 12 x 12 inches and 3/4 inch thick (30 x 30 x 2 cm) would weigh about 12 to 15 pounds (5 to 7 kg).

98

Use the ruler on the back of this book to measure what you find.

OBSIDIAN

WHAT IT LOOKS LIKE

Obsidian is an igneous rock. It is actually lava that cooled too quickly for individual mineral crystals to be visible. If allowed to cool slowly it would have formed granite.

It has a rich, glassy shine. Most commonly, it is pure black. It can also be lighter brown, brown with some black mottling, and black with a golden or silver sheen.

Obsidian fractures (breaks) easily, so it often has sharp edges. Pieces have a swirl pattern where they were split apart.

WHERE TO FIND IT

It is generally found in small outcrops in western states such as California, Oregon, Utah, and Wyoming, and into Mexico. It is not found at all in the eastern states.

Over time, obsidian weathers into a dull black color and can have a pitted surface.

INTERESTING FACTS

If some crystals do form inside the obsidan as it cools, it is called snowflake obsidian. Multi-colored obsidian is called rainbow obsidian. Reddish obsidian is sometimes called fire obsidian.

WHAT IT'S USED FOR

Because it is easily fractured it could be made into tools with razor-sharp points, such as knives and heads on spears and arrows.

Today, obsidian is considered to be a semi-precious stone and is used in making jewelry.

Take your time and don't hurry!

RHYOLITE

WHAT IT LOOKS LIKE

This igneous rock is usually pale gray, pink, or yellow. It is fine-grained and contains some larger fragments of minerals and many smaller crystals. Because the rock was cooled very quickly, the smaller crystals are lined up in stripes (called flow-banding).

Sometimes rhyolite rises up through the ground instead of flowing with magma. The rock might form a mound above the ground.

WHERE TO FIND IT

Thousands of square miles are covered by rhyolite in western Texas, Arizona, California, Mexico, Utah, and Oregon. Reddish rhyolite flows can be seen in the area near Las Vegas on the way to the Hoover Dam.

Italy and Ethiopia are also known for having rhyolite deposits.

WHAT IT'S USED FOR

Because of its strength, rhyolite is sometimes cut into blocks and used for constructing buildings. It also can be used to build roads.

One type of rhyolite, called perlite, is used in some types of sound insulation in buildings. It is also the material added to dirt to make commercial potting soil.

Tell an adult how long you will be gone.

CONGLOMERATE

WHAT IT LOOKS LIKE

Conglomerates are sedimentary rocks composed of coarse gravel fragments cemented together by sand that filled in the spaces between the gravel.

The sand was usually supplied by the movement of water in rivers, streams, and waves. But glaciers and even gravity could help to form conglomerates.

The color of conglomerates depends on the color of the gravel and sand. When the fragments are very colorful, conglomerates may be called "puddingstones."

INTERESTING FACTS

Sometimes, gold was found in "looser" conglomerate formations, so old-time miners knew to look in these areas in California and Alaska.

WHERE TO FIND IT

Conglomerates may be found in rivers and on ocean beaches. They are also common in rocky desert areas where water used to be present.

In Van Horn, Texas, there is a deposit many hundreds of feet thick. Specimens can also be found along the Florida Coast and in Massachusetts, California, Montana, and Oregon.

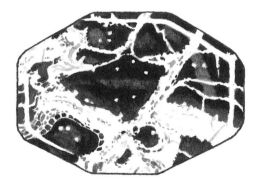

WHAT IT'S USED FOR

Because conglomerates are not very strong, they don't have much commercial use, except for making concrete. But they are sometimes polished as ornamental stone.

Don't drop any litter.

LIMESTONE

WHAT IT LOOKS LIKE

Limestone is made from minerals in the shells and bones of marine animals that are no longer alive. Some limestones are made of whole shells cemented together. This dense sedimentary rock is usually light in color. Some varieties can have shades of pink.

It is usually fine-grained, but some can have coarser grains that are visible.

WHERE TO FIND IT

Limestone beds are formed in tropical marine environments and warm freshwater lakes. Sometimes limestone beds are stacked one on top of another, and you can easily see the layering.

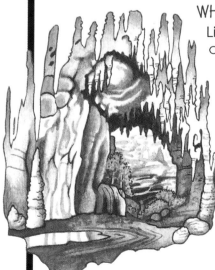

Limestone can also be formed in hot water, especially in areas of hot springs and geysers such as in Yellowstone National Park, Wyoming.

The Canadian Rockies, the pyramids of Egypt, and the White Cliffs of Dover, England, are made of types of limestone.

WHAT IT'S USED FOR

In Bermuda, houses are sometimes made of blocks of coquina, which is a type of limestone composed of shell fragments that have turned to stone.

Limestone is an essential part of mortar, the cement that is spread between bricks to hold them together.

Writing chalk is a kind of limestone!

Take this book and a pencil when you go exploring.

SANDSTONE

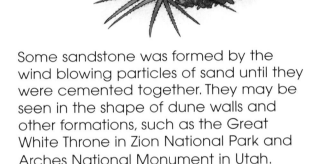

WHAT IT LOOKS LIKE

Sandstone may be white, gray, or yellow-tan to dark red. Most people are used to seeing light tan to brownish-gray specimens.

It is made up of even-sized grains of sand, which are rounded particles of quartz, closely cemented together. It is a sedimentary rock and you usually can clearly see layers.

WHERE TO FIND IT

You may find sandstone almost everywhere near rivers and lakes, especially in forms such as outcroppings, buttes, and mesas.

It also can be found in desert regions where the earth was once covered with water.

INTERESTING FACTS

Some specimens of sandstone contain fossil fragments, footprints, and even the marks of raindrops.

Some sandstone was formed by the wind blowing particles of sand until they were cemented together. They may be seen in the shape of dune walls and other formations, such as the Great White Throne in Zion National Park and Arches National Monument in Utah.

WHAT IT'S USED FOR

Many buildings are made of blocks of sandstone. In the eastern U.S., houses made of sandstone are often called "brownstones."

Sandstone can be crushed and used like sand.

Walk carefully so you do not injure any plants.

SHALE

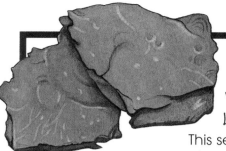

WHAT IT LOOKS LIKE

This sedimentary rock is composed mostly of clay particles. It is also called "mudstone."

Shale can be found anywhere that standing water once existed. Fine particles collect on the bottom of calm water beds and become compressed together. Eventually, other layers form on top.

Distinct layers can be found, sometimes with alternating layers of different colors. Layers can be several feet thick. The layer colors can be gray, to pinkish-purple to dark red, sometimes greenish.

It is a "soft" rock and may break apart when wet. It is easily scratched with a knife and feels smooth and almost greasy to the touch.

INTERESTING FACTS

Under intense heat some shales yield liquid petroleum. But it's very expensive to process. The earth may hold over 42 trillion gallons (159 trillion liters) of this oil.

WHERE TO FIND IT

The best place to see layered mudstone is in dry, desert areas with little vegetation where roadways have been cut through the earth.

It can be found in almost all delta regions, where moving rivers and streams meet calm bodies of water.

The Painted Desert in Arizona is an example of mudstone layering.

WHAT IT'S USED FOR

Shale is used to make bricks. And it can be used to make ceramics and pottery.

To see rocks more easily, carry a plastic magnifying glass with you.

GNEISS

WHAT IT LOOKS LIKE

Gneiss (pronounced "nice") is a metamorphosed, or "changed" rock formed from an igneous rock such as granite. It is made of coarse-grained minerals that are usually visible.

Alternating bands of lighter and darker minerals give it a layered appearance. The layers may look bent or folded. They can be of almost any color, but the more granulated layers are usually lighter in color (white, pink, gray, or tan), while the finer mineral bands are darker (brown or black).

Because gneiss is resistant to weathering, it forms ridges in the landscape that make the terrain look rough and craggy.

WHERE TO FIND IT

Gneiss can be found in the Adirondack regions of New England, south to Georgia. It is also found in the Idaho Batholith area, as well as the Montana and Colorado Rockies.

The region around Great Bear Lake in northwestern Canada is also a good example of a gneiss landscape.

INTERESTING FACTS

Gneiss forms at temperatures of about 1,382 to 1,796°F (750 to 980°C) at depths of 9 to 19 miles (15 to 30 km) beneath the surface.

WHAT IT'S USED FOR

There are not many economic uses for gneiss. It can be used for building purposes when composed of weather-resistant minerals.

Polished slabs may be used as interior decorative stone.

MARBLE

WHAT IT LOOKS LIKE

Marble is actually limestone that has been altered by heat and pressure. Because limestone is usually found near marine or ancient marine environments, that's where you will find marble.

Pure marble is white, but since it is a "changed" rock it may have streaks, bands, or vein-like patterns of darker colors.

You will notice it is fine-grained to medium-grained.

There are also large deposits in Maryland, Vermont, and Georgia.

WHAT IT'S USED FOR

Crushed marble can be used in mixtures of concrete. Statues are often made of marble, and it is used as decoration on the fronts of buildings. When polished, it makes beautiful, decorative stone for columns and tabletops.

The Taj Mahal in India and the Parthenon in Greece are made of marble. So is the Lincoln Memorial in Washington, DC. The Leaning Tower in Pisa, Italy, has many marble panels and columns.

INTERESTING FACTS

In times past, the game of marbles was sometimes played with balls made of polished marble. Today, the marbles are mostly made of glass.

WHERE TO FIND IT

Pure marble deposits have been found in Malaga, Spain. One place where marble can be found in the U.S. is Oregon Caves National Monument.

Explore safely. Go with a partner!

SLATE

WHAT IT LOOKS LIKE

Slate is actually shale that has been compressed over time. Pieces of slate are shiny and flat on the top and bottom surfaces, with a darker gray-to-black color.

When slate breaks, it comes apart in sheets. A cross-cut slope of slate looks like layers and layers of blackboards piled up.

WHERE TO FIND IT

Because it is very resistant to weathering, roofs made of slate tiles can be found throughout the world.

Slate is found in mountains, such as the Alps in Europe and the Appalachians in the U.S.

Slate outcroppings can also be found in some areas of California, Pennsylvania, and New York.

WHAT IT'S USED FOR

Schoolroom blackboards used to be made of whole sheets of slate.

Some slate can also be found in shades of green, red, brown, and purple. Tabletops and floor tiles are often made of these colored slates.

Slate is commonly used to make roofing shingles, especially in hot climates. Flagstone paving rocks are actually slate.

INTERESTING FACTS

The tops of pool tables are made of slate (because it is heavy and has an even surface) and are covered in felt.

Never step into water without first knowing how deep it is.

SCHIST

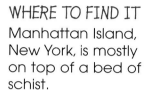

INTERESTING FACTS

Schists often contain other minerals. Garnet crystals are often embedded in schist, as is the mineral talc, from which we get talcum powder.

WHAT IT LOOKS LIKE

Schist can be shale, slate, or basalt that has been metamorphosed.

It usually ranges in color from silvery white, many shades of gray, and yellowish to brownish. When weathered, it can have a rusty color.

Up close, schist seems to be made of compressed, flaky pieces of minerals and rock. It has a layered appearance, although not in bands like gneiss. Schist and gneiss are often found together, and sometimes they are layered with each other.

WHERE TO FIND IT

Manhattan Island, New York, is mostly on top of a bed of schist.

Schist can be found with gneiss in the Idaho Batholith area, as well as New England south to Georgia. It is also commonly found in Canada and Scandinavia.

WHAT IT'S USED FOR

Graphite, used now instead of lead in pencils, can be found in schist.

Depending on the mineral content, blocks of schist may be used as building stones. Sometimes it is crushed and used as gravel.

One type of schist is cut into slabs and used as roofing for houses in the Alps of Europe.

Get permission before going onto someone's land.

GARNET

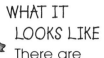

WHAT IT LOOKS LIKE

There are different kinds of this mineral. The ones most people recognize are crimson red to brown in color. Some of them are yellow, green, black, or even clear. Sometimes they may seem to change color in different light.

It was named after the Latin word *granalus* for "pomegranate" because this fruit's seeds are a deep red color.

WHERE TO FIND IT

Garnets are commonly found in igneous and metamorphic rocks such as marble and schist throughout the world.

Gem-quality garnets have been found in Arizona, Utah, Idaho, Alaska, Maine, and North Carolina. Garnets also can be found in many other countries and regions of the world such as Russia, the Czech Republic, Australia, Scandinavia, and South America.

In South Africa, the garnet is called the Cape Ruby.

WHAT IT'S USED FOR

Garnets have been used as a decorative stone since around 5000 B.C. in Egypt. During the Middle Ages they became even more valued as a gemstone.

Some garnets are ground up and used as the abrasive surface on sandpaper.

Garnet is the birthstone for the month of January.

Stay safe! Don't go near the edges of cliffs and outcroppings.

MICA

WHAT IT LOOKS LIKE

Mica is one of the most abundant of rock-forming minerals. It may be found in any of the three types of rock.

It breaks into sheets that can be thinner than a fingernail and translucent. The sheets are somewhat flexible and don't break easily.

There are two forms of mica. Muscovite may be colorless or white to pale yellow to gray. Biotite is usually dark brown to dark green to black because it contains lots of iron. Biotite is less common than Muscovite.

WHERE TO FIND IT

Micas can be found almost everywhere. Utah, California, the Black Hills of South Dakota, and the New England states have large deposits. They are also found in Brazil, India, Scandinavia, and Switzerland.

WHAT IT'S USED FOR

Muscovite was once called Muscovy glass and was used to make the windows of stoves, lanterns, and fuse plugs. It was also used to make electrical insulation in appliances like household irons and toasters.

Some types of house paint contain mica. These paints are usually labeled "fireproof."

INTERESTING FACTS

One crystal of mica that was mined in India weighed 85 tons.

Always wear shoes or boots to protect your feet.

QUARTZ

On the Frederich Mohs scale of hardness, a diamond is a #10 and quartz is a #7. Your fingernail is only a #2.

WHAT IT LOOKS LIKE

This is the most common mineral on Earth. It has a glassy appearance and can be found in almost every color. Rock crystal quartz is colorless and looks like ice. Many specimens are banded.

Quartz forms six-sided crystals (hexagons) and usually has pyramid-shaped ends. Some crystals can be huge, weighing many tons.

It can be found throughout the world. Especially large quartz crystals have been found in Brazil.

Much of the dust in the air consists of quartz.

WHAT IT'S USED FOR

Clear rock crystal quartz generates an electrical charge. It is a very important element of radios, telephones, and wrist watches.

Quartz is the main component of sand. Sand is a major component of glass.

Flint is black quartz. It was used to make sparks that could start fires.

Many different colors of quartz are used as jewelry. Citrine is yellow quartz. Amethyst is a purple gemstone that is a kind of quartz. It is the birthstone for February.

WHERE TO FIND IT

Quartz is an important rock-forming mineral. It can be found in granite, sandstone, and gneiss.

Make Some Rock Candy

If you like sugar, you will really like these crystal "rock" formations.
They are not only fun to make, they taste delicious!

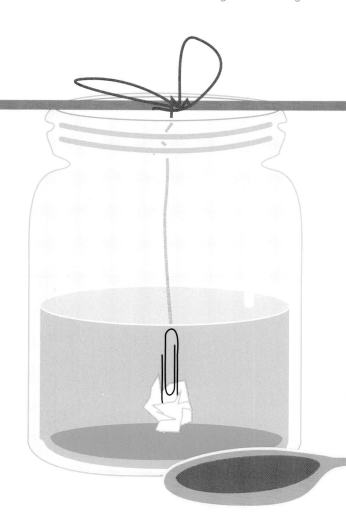

WHAT YOU NEED

- A clean glass jar
- A piece of clean cotton string
- A large paper clip
- A popsicle stick
- Scissors
- 1 cup of water
- A medium saucepan
- A wooden spoon
- 3 or 4 cups of white granulated sugar
- An adult to help you

112

WHAT TO DO

1 Wash and dry the paper clip. Tie it to one end of the string.

2 Tie the other end of the string to the middle of the popsicle stick.

3 Moisten the string with cool water.

4 Rest the popsicle stick across the opening of the jar, letting the string with the paperclip hang down into the jar. Make sure the paperclip does not touch the bottom of the jar.

5 With an adult's help, heat 1 cup of water in the saucepan until it boils. Remove the pan from the heat.

6 When the water stops bubbling, slowly pour the sugar into the water.

7 Stir the water and sugar mixture with the spoon until all or most of the sugar is dissolved.

8 Let the mixture cool for a few minutes, then have an adult pour it into the jar with the string.

9 Set the jar in a place where it won't be disturbed, and you can watch the crystals grow.

The sugar will begin to turn into rock candy in just a few hours. The rock crystals will continue growing for several days. You can eat the candy off the string anytime you wish, but the longer you wait, the bigger the candy will be!

OTHER IDEAS:

• You can add a few drops of flavoring, such as mint or vanilla extract, to the sugar-water mixture before you pour it into the jar.

• You also can add food coloring. Stir one or two drops into the sugar-water before it goes into the jar.

113

FOSSILS

When most plants and animals die, they just rot away, back into the earth, until nothing is left. But sometimes they are completely trapped or covered in mud or sand that turns to rock. Eventually, the rock holding the fossil cracks open or weathers away and the fossil can be found.

Most fossils were sea creatures with shells that are found today in sedimentary rock, such as sandstone and limestone. That means they can be found in areas that used to be water environments. You may find a single fossilized shell or a cluster of shells cemented together.

A whole tree may become a fossil. Its pieces are called petrified wood, and they may be different colors.

Some fossils are not the whole animal or plant, but just its imprint or outline. This kind of fossil may look like a foot print, or tail print, or leaf print.

The oldest fossil ever found is over 3 billion years old! Fossils are still being made every day. Years from now someone will find a shell or plant fossil from today and be able to learn about the things that lived during our lives.

PLANT FOSSILS

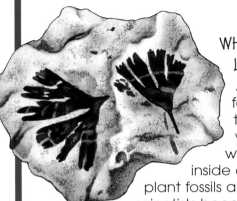

WHAT THEY LOOK LIKE

As rocks formed over thousands of years, plants were trapped inside of them. These plant fossils are valuable to scientists because knowing when the plant lived can help determine the age of the rock.

One way plants may become fossils is by carbonization. This is when the natural oils within the plant seep out, leaving a thin layer of carbon on the rock as it was forming. Commonly found plant fossils are the leaf imprints of eucalyptus, ginkgo, ferns, and palms.

Petrification is another way plants are fossilized. This happens when minerals inside the plant's cells crystallize and become hard. This is how petrified wood is created.

Up close, petrified trees look and feel like solid stone. Because the minerals in petrified wood can contain many colors, it sometimes looks painted or iridescent.

WHERE TO FIND THEM

Plant fossils can be found almost everywhere in many different kinds of rock. Coal beds in particular may contain them. Plant fossils usually are not found in wet, swampy areas, however, because the plants probably deteriorated too quickly to be preserved.

INTERESTING FACTS

Paleontologists are scientists who study fossils. They have even found whole, fossilized pine cones.

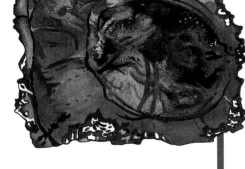

BIVALVES

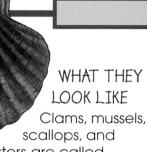

WHAT THEY LOOK LIKE

Clams, mussels, scallops, and oysters are called bivalves because they have left-side and right-side shells. A bivalve's two shells are usually the same size and are nearly identical to each other.

While they are alive, bivalves sometimes burrow into sand or the soft sediment of the water bed. Over time, the sediment may compress into rock, trapping the bivalve inside and forming a fossil.

After the animal inside the shell dies, the muscle holding the two shells together relaxes, and the shells may come apart. So sometimes only half of the bivalve is found.

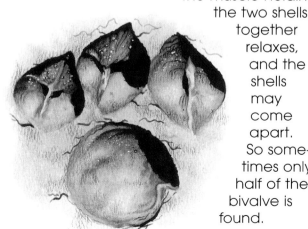

WHERE TO FIND THEM

All bivalves are aquatic, meaning that they live in or near the water. They may be found in both freshwater and saltwater. They are mostly found in shallow areas. Oysters are the most common bivalve found.

Bivalve shells may be tiny—smaller than 1 inch (2.5 cm) across—and some may be large—more than 1 foot (30 cm) across!

Since they live in many different aquatic environments, fossilized bivalves can be found in different kinds of rock, such as sandstone, shale, and limestone.

INTERESTING FACTS

Bivalves have been used as food since prehistoric times. Their fossil records go back over 600 million years.

116

A hat with a brim will protect you from sunburn.

BRACHIOPODS

WHAT THEY LOOK LIKE

Lampshells and spiriferids are examples of brachiopods, which have top and bottom shells.

If you drew an imaginary line down the center of a brachiopod, the two sides would look nearly identical, except that one would be larger. Most brachiopods are less than 5 inches (13 cm) across, but some are almost 1 foot (30 cm) across.

Brachiopods have strong muscles that hold the two shells together, even after the animal inside dies. So you are likely to find a brachiopod fossil with both shells.

WHERE TO FIND THEM

Brachiopods move around less than bivalves, and some cannot move by themselves at all. They rely on the water's currents to transport them. Some brachiopods attach themselves to the floor of the ocean and remain in that one place their whole lives. A few brachiopods burrow into the muddy bottom.

Brachiopods sometimes join together. Whole groups of fossilized brachiopods have been found cemented in rock. Limestone, shale, and sandstone are just some of the rocks in which they have been found.

INTERESTING FACTS

When brachiopods find a surface to live on, they grab on with a "foot," called a pedicle.

Don't approach or touch any wild animals you may see.

BRYOZOANS

WHAT THEY LOOK LIKE

Living bryozoans can be found on most seashores, as well as in deep water. They are called aquatic "moss animals." Each individual bryozoan is only about 1 mm long. It would take twenty-five of them to measure 1 inch (2.5 cm).

Some bryozoans attach to each other and form groups called colonies that look like fan-shaped, lacy leaves. Other colonies look like little branched twigs. A whole bryozoan colony may be only 1 or 2 inches (2.5 to 5 cm) across. Larger colonies can be 2 feet (61 cm) across.

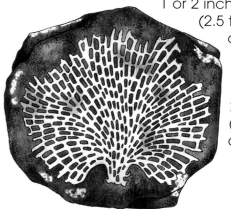

WHERE TO FIND THEM

Fossilized bryozoans are often found in specimens of shale. Thousands of years ago, many colonies of bryozoans inhabited the oceans. They looked like a mossy field swaying in the water currents. As layer upon layer of sediment formed on the ocean floor, they hardened and compressed into shale, or became limestone. The colonies of bryozoans were trapped between the layers and became fossilized.

Bryozoans usually attach themselves to hard objects, such as rocks, in shallow waters. They also may attach themselves to ships, pilings, piers, and docks.

INTERESTING FACTS

The common name of a bryozoan may come from its appearance, such as porcupine, bushy, hairy, and black-speckled.

Use patience and sharp eyesight to find fossils.

TRILOBITES

WHAT THEY LOOK LIKE

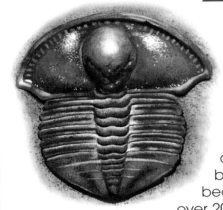

Trilobites were very common marine animals before they became extinct over 200 million years ago. Scientists believe there were thousands of species, or kinds, of trilobites. Some were very tiny and some grew as long as 3 feet (0.9 m).

They had many legs and hard outer shells, called exoskeletons, that were either smooth or edged with spines.

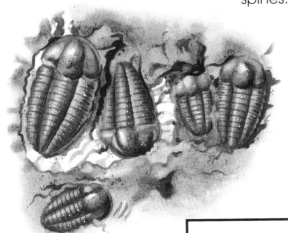

Trilobites had to shed their outer shells in order to grow. So some trilobite fossils are not the entire animal, but only their old shell.

WHERE TO FIND THEM

Trilobites lived in shallow waters throughout the world. They were mostly bottom-dwellers, where they could burrow into the sand and mud to hide or find food. Some fossils show the trail and tracks a trilobite left as it moved along.

When trilobites defended themselves, they would roll up into a ball. Some have been found in rock this way. Also, trilobites were very social, and groups of them have been found fossilized together. Limestone and shale are the best rocks for finding trilobite fossils. Billions of them have been found in the Wheeler Shale Formation in Utah.

INTERESTING FACTS

Trilobites lived and became extinct even before dinosaurs roamed the earth. They are ancient relatives of today's horseshoe crabs, spiders, and cockroaches.

Stay away from poison ivy and poison oak when you explore.

Create Your Own Fossil

You can make a "secret" fossil by yourself. Or you can make fossils
with your family or friends. Even your pet can have a fossil of its own!

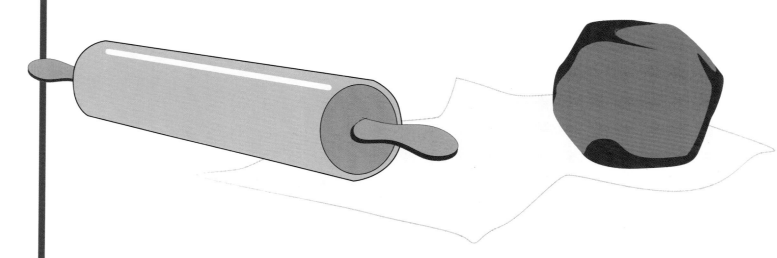

WHAT YOU NEED

▼

- Modeling clay
- Newspapers
- Waxed paper
- An old rolling pin
- A pencil or toothpick

WHAT TO DO

▼

1 Cover the top of a table with newspapers.

2 Put a large piece of waxed paper right in front
of you on the table.

3 Squeeze the clay in your hands until it becomes
soft. Then set it on the waxed paper.

4 With your hands, roll the clay into a smooth ball.

5 Press the ball flat, removing any air bubbles.

6 Make the clay into any shape you like, such as a square, rectangle, triangle, or circle.

7 Use the rolling pin to make the clay flat and even. Use your hands to help keep the shape. Do not make it too thin or too big. You should be able to pick it up without bending or tearing it.

8 Gently press your hand into the clay deep enough to leave a good print. Slowly lift up your hand. If you pressed hard enough you should be able to see lines and fingerprints in the clay.

9 Next, use the pencil or toothpick to "write" your name and the date you made the fossil.

10 Set the fossil in a place where it can completely dry out. It may take several days.

Now you're ready to turn your clay into a true fossil! Find a place outside where you have permission to dig. Pick a spot that usually stays dry and is not near water. Dig a deep hole and carefully place your fossil inside. Cover it with dirt, gently packing the dirt so there are no air spaces. If no one disturbs your fossil, someone may find it hundreds of years from now.

OTHER IDEAS:

• You can also press leaves into the clay to make plant fossils. Use leaves that are thick and sturdy and that don't tear easily. Choose leaves that have thick veins or interesting edges.

• If you want to keep your fossil, you can paint it and use it as a paperweight or give it as a gift to someone special.

ARROWHEADS & ARTIFACTS

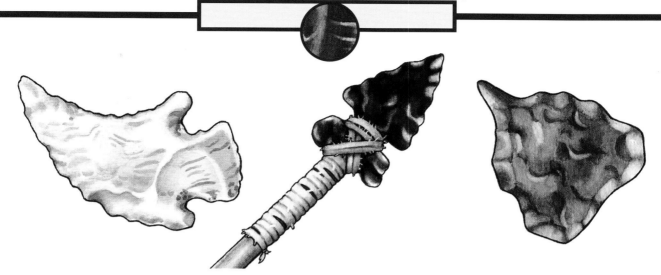

When early people needed tools and weapons, they made many of them from stones and sticks that they found close to where they lived. For almost as long as humans have been on the Earth, they have made tools and weapons in order to build shelter, hunt for food, and defend themselves.

In North America, there are clues to how the early Native Americans lived. These clues are found every time a person discovers a kind of Indian artifact.

Different tribes in different areas used different materials and different shapes for their tools and weapons. Many items were formed from igneous rock because it is very strong. Some were made from softer sedimentary rock because it could be sharpened into a point.

Heavy rocks were often used for axes or hammers. Lighter and smaller rocks were used for more delicate work, such as poking holes in pieces of an animal hide to sew them together for clothing.

KNIVES

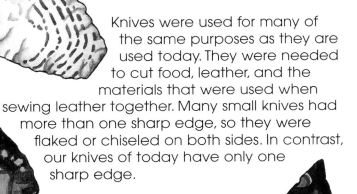

Knives were used for many of the same purposes as they are used today. They were needed to cut food, leather, and the materials that were used when sewing leather together. Many small knives had more than one sharp edge, so they were flaked or chiseled on both sides. In contrast, our knives of today have only one sharp edge.

Some knives were notched so they could be attached to wooden handles. Early knives were oblong shaped or pear shaped with one end wider to grasp it with the hand. Many of them were about 4 to 5 inches (10 to 13 cm) long. Some were as long as 9 inches (22 cm). Large knives usually only had one very sharp edge.

Even when found today, many ancient knives are still sharp enough to be used. Sometimes knives are found with coarse edges, or with serrations that look like tiny teeth. These knives were used as saws.

Don't put your hand into any hole or burrow. It may be an animal's home.

123

ARROWHEADS

Most arrowheads found today are between 1/2 inch (1.25 cm) and 2 inches (5 cm) long. It is likely that small ones were attached to small sticks for hunting birds. Large ones on stronger pieces of wood were probably used to hunt larger animals.

Most regions had just one type of flint, and most arrowheads found in that area were made in one shape. Because flint can be white, gray, red, or black, arrowheads can be different colors.

Arrowheads were usually made out of a hard sedimentary rock called flint. There are different types of flint in North America so you may find different types of arrowheads in different parts of the continent.

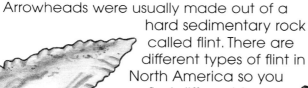

An arrowhead has three parts. The sharp end is called the tip, or point. The wide middle section is called the body, or face. The square end is called the base or bottom. Often when a person finds an arrowhead in a field or near a stream, the arrowhead is broken. It might be missing the tip or base, or both.

When exploring at night, take a flashlight.

When pieces of flint chip off, the edges are sharp. Those edges of the arrowhead are beveled, or sloped, by carefully striking it with another very hard rock. This makes the edge thin and even sharper.

Many arrowheads have a notch on each side where the body and base meet. Arrowheads are notched in different ways. For example, some arrowheads are side-notched while others are bottom-notched or corner-notched. And others may be notched in more than one place.

Pay attention to everything around you.

SPEAR POINTS

An artifact that is larger than 2 inches (5 cm) and looks like an arrowhead is called a spear point. It may be even longer than 3 inches (7.5 cm). Spears were used in hunting animals for food. They were made of long pieces of wood with a sharp "point" attached to one end. Spears could be thrown or carried by hand.

Most spear points do not have notches for attaching to the spear shaft. The edges away from the sharp end were usually ground smooth so they could be attached to wooden spears without cutting through the binding material. In addition to flint, some spear points were made of obsidian, quartz, or buffalo bone.

If spear points or arrowheads became chipped or broken during use, they were often remade into other small tools such as knives or scrapers.

INTERESTING FACTS

Spear points were invented several hundred years before arrow-heads. They date back as far as 7500 B.C.

Tell an adult where you are going, or take one with you.

AXES

One of the largest artifacts you may find is a stone axe. These were often made out of granite, slate, or iron ore, but not flint. Other harder stones were used to grind the axe stone, forming a wedge shape with one sharp side.

The large groove near the blunt end of the axe was used to help fasten it to a handle. The groove could be shallow or deep, wide or narrow, straight or angled.

The weight of an axe may range from 1 pound (0.45 kg) to 20 pounds (9 kg). The size could be small for easy jobs, or large for difficult jobs. Their main purpose was to cut and chop wood for fires and building materials. They were also important in constructing shelters. The blunt or back end of a heavy axe was sometimes used as a hammer.

Small axes without grooves were used without a handle and are called "celts." These hand axes were very smooth for a more comfortable grip. They were used for chopping smaller objects like branches and twigs.

INTERESTING FACTS

Axes are commonly found in the Midwest where there were vast forests. They were sometimes used to form a dug-out, or canoe, from the trunk of a fallen tree.

127

Wear a hat and use sunscreen to protect yourself from the sun.

DRILLS AND AWLS

In their everyday lives, early people needed to make holes in animal hides, softer stones, and wood. In order to do this they made tools that they could use to puncture through these materials.

A drill was usually notched to attach it to the end of a stick. To make a hole, the pointed end was placed on the material and the stick was rotated back and forth by rubbing it between the hands.

Drills were often made of broken arrowheads or bones of animals. Because a drill is much narrower than the body of an arrowhead, it was perfect for recycling into this new use. Sometimes they were made of petrified wood. They could be as long as 4 inches (10 cm).

Awls can be as long as drills but they are not as narrow. They are more triangular in shape and have no notches. Awls were almost always made of flint and they were made to be held in the hand. A depression was often carved in one side for the thumb of the person who was using it. This made it easier to grip.

128

Use insect repellent to protect yourself.

SCRAPERS

Scrapers were used in preparing many kinds of food, as well as hides for clothing and shelter. They were also used to make other tools out of animal bones.

Pieces of quartz and flint were used as scrapers. They have one edge that is much thinner than the other edges. To make a scraper sharper, it would be flaked only on one side, leaving the other side smooth.

They may be as small as a thumbnail or large enough to be gripped in the whole hand. Scrapers were often oval or round. Different shapes worked better for different uses.

An indentation for a thumb is often seen where the person using the scraper would need to grip it. The handle side is smooth.

Scrapers were not usually resharpened. When one scraper became dull from the work, Indians simply made another to continue the job.

Take this book with you and have fun!

129

Design a Friendship Necklace

WHAT TO DO

1 Lay the three long pieces of yarn together, stretched out straight.

2 Tie them together in a knot at one end.

3 Braid the three pieces of yarn, starting at the knot end. Make sure the braid is not too loose. When you finish the braid, tie the loose ends together in another knot.

4 Wrap the middle of the short piece of yarn around the arrowhead at the notches. Criss-cross and tie the yarn to make sure the arrowhead is tied tight.

5 Tightly tie the ends of the short yarn to the center of the braided yarn, so the arrowhead hangs down a little.

6 Tie the ends of the braid together to make a necklace that you can slip over your head.

Everyone will admire your necklace. You can give it as a gift to a special friend. Or you could make two matching necklaces for you and your pal as a sign of friendship!

WHAT YOU NEED

- 3 pieces of yarn, each about 36 inches (1 m) long
- 1 piece of yarn about 15 inches (38 cm) long
- An arrowhead that's clean and dry
- Scissors

OTHER IDEAS:

- Instead of yarn, you can use ribbon, string, cloth strips, or long shoelaces for your necklace.

- You can also use shorter pieces and make a bracelet, key chain, or bookmark.

Make an Arrowhead Display

WHAT YOU NEED

- Soap, water, and an old toothbrush
- A soft towel
- An empty egg carton
- Cotton balls
- Small pieces of paper for note tags
- A pen or pencil
- Liquid glue

WHAT TO DO

1 Use the toothbrush with soap and water to gently clean your arrowheads. Wipe them dry with the towel.

2 Place a cotton ball in each of the egg carton holes. Lay one arrowhead on top of each cotton ball.

3 Make a note on a piece of paper for each arrowhead. It could say where and when you found it.

4 Put a dot of glue on the back of the paper. Press it on the cotton beside its arrowhead.

Now your collection won't get lost or damaged. And it's ready to show to your family and friends!

OTHER IDEAS:

- If your arrowheads are too big to fit in the holes of an egg carton, you can use a shoe box with a lid. The cotton balls can cover the entire bottom of the box, and the arrowheads can be placed on them as they will fit.

- You can make another display box for rocks or other treasures you find.

SCRAPBOOK

Rocks, Fossils and Arrowheads

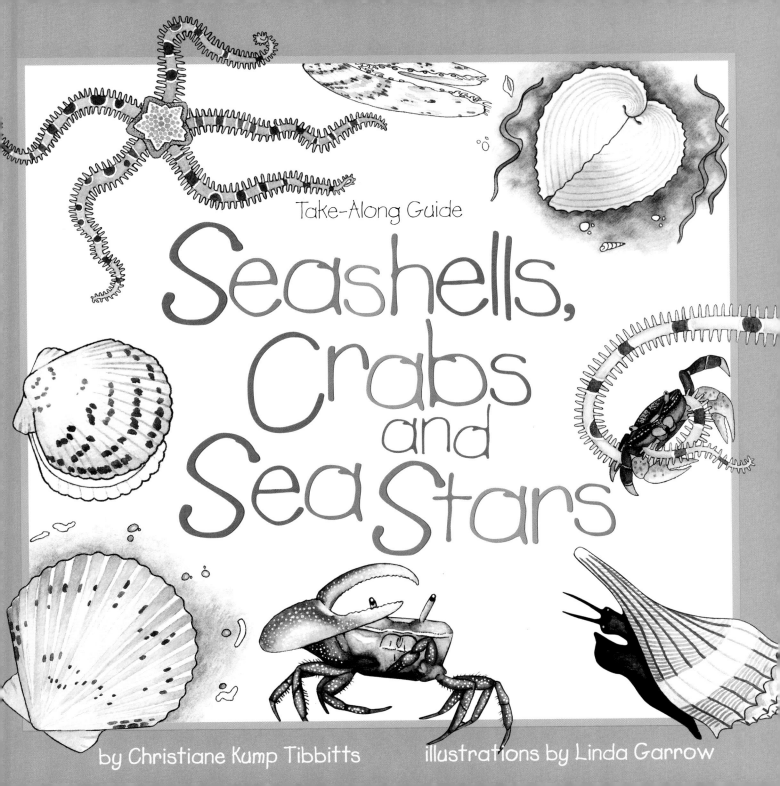

Take-Along Guide

Seashells, Crabs and Sea Stars

by Christiane Kump Tibbitts   illustrations by Linda Garrow

INTRODUCTION

As a wave sweeps the beach, tiny clams pop up. On a mud flat, a crab runs sideways and zips down a hole. In a rocky tide pool, a sea star moves slowly. Amazing animals live at the seashore. You can find them—with sharp eyes and patience.

Seashores can be sandy, muddy or rocky. They can be pounded by waves or protected in bays. A place where fresh water from rivers or streams mixes with salt water is called an estuary. Some places have salt marshes or swamps. Each kind of shore is home to many animals and plants.

The seashore is always changing. This Take-Along Guide and its activities will help you know some amazing seashore creatures. You can use the ruler on the back of this book to measure the interesting things you find. You can bring a pencil and draw what you see in the scrapbook.

Always remember, if a shell feels full, or you can see something inside, the animal is alive and should not be disturbed.

Discover and have fun in the world of Seashells, Crabs and Sea Stars!

SEASHELLS

Seashells are really the outer coverings of animals known as mollusks. Snails, clams and oysters are just a few examples. These mollusks make a chalky juice that hardens into a shell. The shell protects the mollusk's soft, squishy body. As the animal grows, it makes its shell larger. When mollusks die, their empty shells wash up on the beach for you to find.

Snails make shells that twist in a spiral. A snail glides around on a big, slimy foot. Many snails have a hard plate on the foot. When the snail hides in its shell, this plate closes the opening like a door.

A snail's head has two feelers and two eyes. The snail's tongue has rows of tiny, raspy teeth. It is called a radula.

Clams have two shells that open and close like a suitcase. The shells are joined at the top. A clam has a strong foot to burrow in sand or mud.

Some other kinds of mollusks live fastened to hard places. Most of these animals do not have heads or eyes.

LEWIS' MOON SNAIL

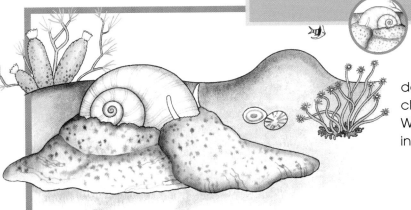

A moon snail eats about four clams a day. The snail wraps its huge foot around a clam and spreads strong acid on the shell. With its radula, the moon snail bores a hole into the shell and sucks out the clam.

This snail was named for Meriwether Lewis. He found it when he explored the Pacific Coast. Under a moving hump of sand, a moon snail plows along on its giant foot. The foot is so large, it looks like it could never fit in the shell, but it does.

This moon snail's thick shell grows to about 3 inches long and 5 inches wide. The outside is yellow-white to pale brown. The inside is gray. The snail's foot is gray. It is flat and oval. It is about three times as long as the shell.

Lewis' moon snails can be found in sandy or muddy bays from British Columbia, Canada to California. Look in the sand near the low tide line for a wide track or a low hump.

The best times to explore are low tide or after storms.

FLAT PERIWINKLE

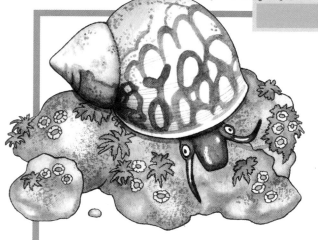

A flat periwinkle is about 1/2 inch high and just as wide. The shell is brown-gray with white spots. It often has many flat, worn places, but we don't know why. Inside the shell is dark brown with a white band on the bottom.

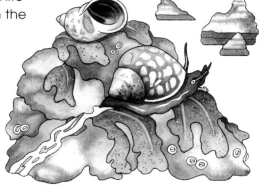

The flat periwinkle climbs rocks above the high tide line, higher than any other marine mollusk on the Pacific Coast. Over many years, flat periwinkles left the sea and slowly learned to breathe air. Flat periwinkles live out of the water most of the time. They can still breathe under water, too.

Flat periwinkles slide slowly across rocks on a trail of slime. This comes out of a slit in the snail's foot. A periwinkle moves like a skater on ice. The snail glides on one side of its foot, then the other. Flat periwinkles wander, scraping seaweed off rocks with their radulas. These snails may be found feeding even during low tide.

Flat periwinkles can be found from Washington to California.

Before exploring, check the newspaper for low and high tide times—they change each day.

SALTMARSH SNAIL

Saltmarsh snails eat rotting marsh plants. The snail uses its radula to scrape them off the mud. You can find saltmarsh snails in southern California salt marshes. The snails live near the high tide line among pickleweed. At low tide they hide under rotting plants or dig into the mud.

This snail has a lung and breathes air. Saltmarsh snails drown if they're under water too long. They somehow know when high tide will be. The snails climb marsh grass before the water gets high. Some tides are very high. A saltmarsh snail has no lid to close its shell. So the snail holds its breath until the tide drops. A saltmarsh snail can hold its breath about an hour!

This snail is about 1 inch high and 1/2 inch wide. Its thin shell is brown with white spiral bands. It is white inside. The snail is gray.

SPECIAL WARNING

Don't go wading without an adult.

ATLANTIC OYSTER DRILL

Atlantic oyster drills like to eat oysters. First, the oyster drill crawls on top of the oyster shell and feels around for the best place to drill. Acid comes out of the snail's foot and eats into the shell. Then the oyster drill scrapes with its radula. For three days, the oyster drill keeps spreading acid and scraping. Finally there is a small, straight hole through the shell. The oyster drill uses its long tongue to eat the oyster.

The inside of the shell is purple, white, yellow or brown. The snail is creamy white.

Atlantic oyster drills live on oyster beds, rocks and docks in the saltier parts of estuaries and on bay and ocean shores. You can find them from Nova Scotia, Canada to Florida, and from Washington to California.

The Atlantic oyster drill is about 1 inch long and 1/2 inch wide. The shell is spindle-shaped and has ribs crossed with spiral cords. The shell is gray, tan or yellow-white with brown spiral bands.

Wear old sneakers to protect your feet from sharp objects.

LIGHTNING WHELK

A small lightning whelk fits in your hand. But a big one is more than a handful. The shell grows about 3 to 16 inches long. The snail's foot is black.

A snail's shell grows in an ever-larger spiral. You can see this at the top of a shell. On most snail shells the spiral twists to the right. On some, it twists to the left. The lightning whelk is a left-handed shell.

A lightning whelk likes to eat hard-shelled clams. This whelk often has a battered shell from banging against clams to crack them open. Then the whelk scrapes the clam out with its radula.

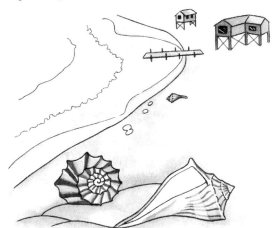

The lightning whelk's shell is thick. It is wide on one end, and comes to a point at the other end. The shell is yellow to gray-white. It has thin red-brown "lightning" streaks from end to end. The inside is white.

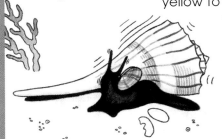
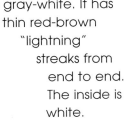

Lightning whelks live along sandy beaches from New Jersey to Florida and Texas. They are also found in the saltier parts of estuaries.

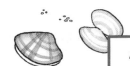

Always put rocks back the way you found them.

CAYENNE KEYHOLE LIMPET

A cayenne keyhole limpet is oval. It is 1/2 to 2 inches long. The shell is ribbed and white, cream, gray or pink. The inside is shiny and blue-gray or white. The snail is creamy white.

Keyhole limpets are most active at night during high tide. A limpet wanders over rocks, scraping off seaweed with its radula. At low tide, each limpet returns to a home spot it has chosen.

A cayenne (pronounced "KI-EN") keyhole limpet's shell looks like a small volcano. The hole on top is shaped like a keyhole. This gives this limpet its name. A keyhole limpet pulls water in under its shell to breathe. Water and wastes go out the hole on top.

The snail's strong foot clamps down like a suction cup. Its cone-shaped shell is pressed down even tighter when heavy waves hit.

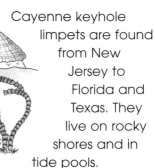

Cayenne keyhole limpets are found from New Jersey to Florida and Texas. They live on rocky shores and in tide pools.

Bring a small shovel and plastic bags for collecting things.

BLACK KATY CHITON

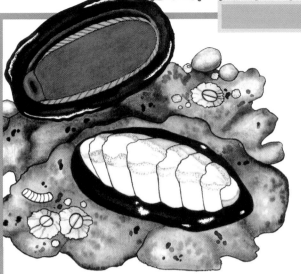

A chiton can hang onto a rock like a suction cup by raising its body up inside its girdle. If it loses its grip, a chiton curls up in a little ball, safe inside its armor.

The black Katy chiton (pronounced "KI-TON") is 1-1/2 to 3 inches long. It is covered by a row of eight gray or blue-white plates of shell. Each plate is curved and shaped like a boomerang. The plates are part of the soft animal's back. They overlap each other, forming an oval shield. Around the edge is a shiny black, stretchy band of muscle called the girdle.

Under all this armor is a very simple mollusk. Most of it is a large, strong red foot. At one end of the body is a mouth with a radula.

A black Katy chiton is a dull color like rock. This helps the animal hide from enemies. Black Katy chitons move around in the daytime, chewing seaweed off rocks. You can find them on rocky shores from Alaska to California.

A snorkeling mask placed on top of the water in a tide pool helps you see into it.

BLUE MUSSEL

Blue mussels live tied to rocks and hard places, anchored with silky but tough threads. The mussel makes sticky stuff with its foot. The sticky stuff forms threads that harden in seawater. The mussel attaches these threads to rock. Waves toss mussels like little boats. But their anchor lines hold.

A blue mussel looks like a long triangle with rounded corners. One corner is pointed, where the mussel's two shells join. The blue mussel grows to be about 4 inches long and 2 inches high. The shells are thin and shiny blue-black. Inside they are pearly blue-white and purple. The mussel's foot is brown.

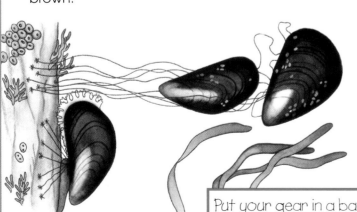

You can find blue mussels from the Arctic to South Carolina, and from Alaska to California. They anchor to anything solid—rocks, docks and even boats. Crowds of blue mussels live in bays and estuaries. These mussels also live on ocean shores among seaweeds and in tide pools.

Put your gear in a backpack or water-proof bag to leave your hands free.

EASTERN OYSTER

The eastern oyster grows to be about 2 to 10 inches long. The shell is oval, with sharp edges. It is thick and wrinkled. The outside is gray. The inside is white with purple. The animal inside is gray.

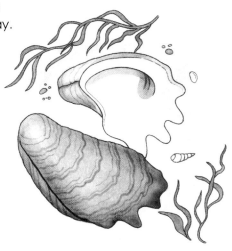

When oysters are young, they find a hard spot to stick to and stay there for life. Other oysters settle nearby. They grow. New oysters settle on top of them. In time, an oyster city of many layers rises up.

No two oysters are alike. A growing oyster is shaped by what it lays on. Its two shells are uneven. The bottom shell is cupped. The top one is flat. An oyster opens its shell to strain tiny plants and animals from water. At low tide, oysters close.

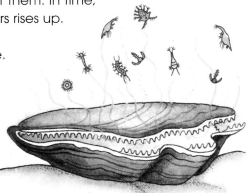

Oysters like a mix of salty and fresh water. They live in shallow water in estuaries, salt marshes and mangrove swamps. You can find eastern oysters along the shore from the Gulf of the St. Lawrence River to the Gulf of Mexico.

Sunscreen, layered clothes and a sun hat keep you comfortable.

COON OYSTER

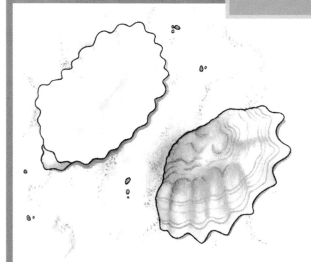

A coon oyster has hooks to hold onto things. Its bottom shell grows spines like little fingers. Coon oysters grip the arched roots of red mangrove trees. This way, the oysters stay above the mud. At low tide, they are uncovered by water. Early Spanish explorers thought these oysters climbed trees!

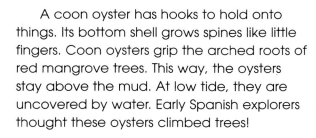

Coon oysters strain the food they eat from the water. They are food, too. At low tide at night raccoons eat them. That is how coon oysters got their name.

A coon oyster is about 1 to 3 inches long. The two shells are roughly oval. They are yellow-white, rosy or brown. The inside is green or white and purple. Big, uneven ridges make a zigzag around the shell's edge. Sometimes coon oysters cling to each other in a bunch. They also live on brush in shallow water. Coon oysters are found from North Carolina to Florida.

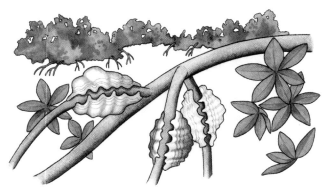

SPECIAL WARNING Watch out for alligators and snakes in mangrove swamps, and go with a guide.

COMMON JINGLE SHELL

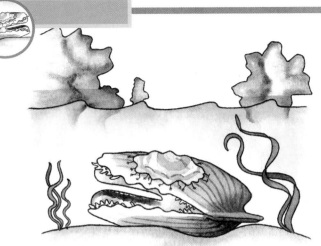

This round shell is so thin you can see through it. Jingle shells look like toenails. Sometimes jingle shells are called "mermaid's toenails."

The common jingle shell is pearly white, gold, apricot, silvery gray or black. It is about 1 to 2 inches long. Jingle shells come in pairs. The two shells are not the same. The top one is cupped and the bottom one is flat. The bottom shell has a hole. Through this hole, the animal sticks itself to a hard place.

These threads harden in seawater. The jingle is stuck for life in the place it has chosen. As a jingle grows, its shell becomes shaped to fit its home.

Jingle shells live stuck to rocks, docks and other shells like oysters. Sometimes jingles also stick to boats or horseshoe crabs. A jingle fastens itself by spinning sticky threads with its foot.

Common jingle shells can be found from Nova Scotia, Canada to Florida and Texas. You can find these shells on sandy or rocky beaches.

Be careful climbing on rocks—they can be slippery.

COQUINA CLAM

Coquinas move with the tides. From time to time, all the clams pop out of the sand at once. They ride a wave to a new place on the beach and dig in.

These clams are about the size of dried beans. Coquinas (pronounced "KO-KE-NA") live jam-packed just beneath the sand. There could be 1,000 of them under your feet!

Coquinas are 1/2 to 1 inch long. They come in a rainbow of colors. The outside is white with bands or sunrays of pink, purple, blue, orange or yellow. The inside is white with yellow, purple or pink.

Each coquina digs by stretching its pointed foot down in the sand. Then the clam pulls in its smooth shell. The triangle shape helps the shell slide in easily.

Coquina clams live where the waves pound sandy beaches from New York to Florida and Texas. You may find bunches of open coquina shells still joined together. Some people call these butterfly shells.

SPECIAL WARNING Stay away from jellyfish—their stingers are poisonous.

NORTHERN QUAHOG

Northern quahogs live buried just beneath the sand and mud. When you step close, a quahog squirts water as it digs down to get away. This clam can dig fast with its strong foot.

Long ago, Native Americans admired these shells and made them into beads. This was done by drilling and polishing pieces of shell. Belts of these beads were valuable. Some people call the quahog (pronounced "KWA-HOG") the hard-shelled clam because it has a thick shell.

Quahogs strain tiny plants and animals from seawater. This also helps the quahog breathe. An adult quahog pumps through more than 15 quarts of water an hour.

The northern quahog is oval. It is about 3 to 6 inches long. The two shells look the same. Each is gray-yellow outside, often with brown. Lines run across the shell. The inside is white and purple.

Look for northern quahogs on tidal flats in bays and along ocean shores. These clams can be found from Quebec to Florida and Texas, and in California.

Protect the seashore. Don't take live animals or plants.

151

CALICO SCALLOP

A scallop has over 30 bright blue eyes. They peek out around the edge of its shell. The eyes see only shadows, but help the scallop escape from enemies.

The calico scallop has two round, cupped shells. One is flatter than the other. Each shell is about 1 to 3 inches long. Ridges on the shell make a "scallop" pattern at the edge. Calico scallops are spotted or mottled. They may be any mix of white, yellow, brown, orange, red or purple. The inside is white.

Most mollusks move slowly, or not at all. But scallops can swim. A scallop swims by clapping its shells together. Water squirts out one side, pushing the scallop the other way. A scallop can jet three feet at a time! They swim to keep from getting buried in mud.

Calico scallops lie on their flat side on sand or mud in shallow to deep water. You can find their shells on sandy beaches from North Carolina to Florida and Texas.

Some places are muddy,
so be sure to wear boots.

HEART COCKLE

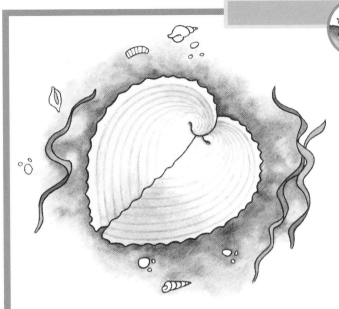

Cockles burrow in sand or mud, but not very deep. When an enemy comes near, a cockle leaps away. It bends its strong foot and pushes off the sand. A cockle can jump several inches at a time.

A cockle has two shells that look the same. Each shell is oval to almost round. It is deeply cupped with thick ridges. The shell edge looks ruffled. From the side, a cockle looks like a heart.

The heart cockle is 2 to 5-1/2 inches long. The shell's outside is gray with a thin, flaky yellow-orange or yellow-brown covering. The inside is yellow-white. The cockle's foot is bright yellow and shaped like a hatchet.

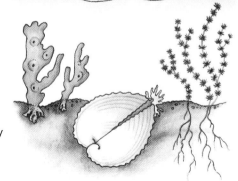

Heart cockles live in quiet bays and estuaries. They also live along open shores. Cockles can be found from the low-tide line to deep water. Look for holes in the sand or mud. Sometimes a cockle lies above the sand. But it can burrow in seconds. Heart cockles are found from Alaska to California.

Don't leave litter on the shore—
it can hurt or kill animals.

JINGLE-JANGLE WIND CHIME

Seashells are not only beautiful, but they can also make music in the wind. Many seashells have holes in them. The bottom parts of jingle shells grow with holes in them. But snails like oyster drills and moon snails bore the holes in other shells. These are shells you can use to make this wind chime.

WHAT YOU NEED

▼

- 12 feet of string
- a washable marker
- a 12-inch ruler or a yardstick
- scissors
- lots of seashells, each with a hole in it
- a piece of driftwood or a thick stick

An adult can help you hang your wind chime outdoors where everyone can admire it and listen to the music!

WHAT TO DO

▼

1 Cut 4 pieces of string each 3 feet long.

2 Mark 3 strings 8 inches from one end.

3 Put one string through the hole of one shell. Slide it to the 8-inch mark. Tie a knot. Below it, tie on another shell close to the first one. Tie on shells the rest of the way down the string. Do the same for the other 2 marked strings.

4 Tie one end of each string of shells to the piece of wood.

5 Push the strings close together so the shells touch.

6 Tie the last piece of string to the piece of wood to make a loop for hanging.

SEASHORE RUBBINGS

Many things are fun to touch at the seashore. Bumpy shells, smooth pebbles, twisty driftwood and seaweed are a few things you can collect to do this fun activity.

WHAT YOU NEED

▼

- some objects to rub over
- tracing paper
- transparent tape
- crayons (with the paper covers off)
- scissors

WHAT TO DO

▼

1 Put an object on a flat place where you have room to work. If you can, tape down the object.

2 With one hand, hold the paper down tightly over the object.

3 With the other hand, rub a crayon on the paper over the object. Use the side of the crayon and rub hard. Try to make all the edges look clear and sharp.

4 Try many different kinds of things. You can have just one object on the paper or you can have several.

You can make a picture with rubbings. You can create bookmarks and letter paper. Or you can use paper with rubbings all over it as gift wrap.

CRABS

Crabs, like seashells, have outer shells to protect their bodies. A crab's shell has many plates joined together. The shell does not get bigger as the crab starts to grow. When its shell becomes tight, the crab grows a new one under it. Then, the old shell splits and the crab wriggles out of it. After three days its new, soft shell becomes hard.

A crab has two eyes on stalks to see in all directions. Between the eyes are two pairs of feelers. Crabs have 5 pairs of legs. The front pair has claws used to grab food and for fighting. The other legs are used for walking or swimming. A crab can grow new legs to replace ones it loses!

Some crabs live in the sea. Others live on land. Crabs eat seaweed and small sea animals.

Barnacles are not true crabs, but are related more to them than to any other animal. Barnacles are the only crab cousins that live attached to the same place for life. Horseshoe crabs are actually more closely related to spiders!

GHOST CRAB

A ghost crab can run fast—up to five feet per second! This crab runs on the tips of its eight long legs. It can run forward, backward or sideways. It can turn and switch legs while running in the same direction.

A ghost crab burrows in damp sand. The crab warns enemies away by making a creaking sound. It does this by rubbing its two claws together. Before leaving its burrow, the crab peeks out. Its eyes are on long stalks.

At night, groups of ghost crabs come out. They hunt small animals like mole crabs and coquina clams. Ghost crabs also eat dead plants and animals washed on the beach.

These crabs live on quiet, sandy beaches from Rhode Island to Florida and Texas.

Ghost crabs are pale gray or yellow like sand. Its body is 2 inches wide, but its legs make it look bigger. The legs are about 4 to 6 inches long.

SPECIAL WARNING Watch out for rising tides!

LONG-CLAWED HERMIT CRAB

When a hermit crab grows too large for its shell, the crab looks for a bigger shell. It lifts and tries on many empty shells. Finally it slips out of its old shell into a new one.

This crab has a hard shell only on the front part of its body. Its back end is soft, and easy to attack. So a hermit crab wears an empty snail shell like a suit of armor. Its claws and front legs stick out of the shell. One claw is bigger than the other. When the crab hides inside its shell, the bigger claw blocks the opening.

The long-clawed hermit crab is about 1/2 inch long and 1/2 inch wide. It is tan, lavender-gray or green-white. It has a tan-gray stripe on its big claw.

The long-clawed hermit crab lives in shallow to deep water on sand, mud, rock and in seaweeds. It lives along ocean or bay shores from Nova Scotia, Canada to Florida and Texas.

Salt marshes are fragile—
explore carefully.

SAND FIDDLER CRAB

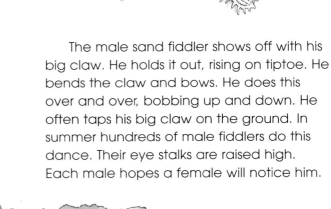

A male sand fiddler crab has one claw that is much bigger than the other. The big claw is longer than his whole body! He looks as if he were holding a fiddle, or violin.

The male sand fiddler shows off with his big claw. He holds it out, rising on tiptoe. He bends the claw and bows. He does this over and over, bobbing up and down. He often taps his big claw on the ground. In summer hundreds of male fiddlers do this dance. Their eye stalks are raised high. Each male hopes a female will notice him.

This crab's body is about 1 inch long and 1 inch wide. The top of the crab is lavender. Brown, gray or black spots are on the sides. The male's big claw is blue, lavender or red-brown. The female fiddler is darker and duller.

Sand fiddler crabs are found from Massachusetts to Florida and Texas. They live in sandy areas of salt marshes nearest the sea. These crabs also live on sandy bay beaches.

Use insect repellent to protect yourself from biting flies.

HORSESHOE CRAB

Horseshoe crabs lived on earth even before dinosaurs!

A horseshoe crab has one large eye on each side of its shell and two smaller eyes in front. It can see only light and dark. A horseshoe crab is 12 inches wide and 24 inches long. Its name comes from its shape.

This crab's long, pointed tail is harmless. If the crab gets turned over, it uses its tail to turn itself right side up.

A horseshoe crab has six pairs of legs. Between the last three pairs is its mouth. The first two legs have small claws. The other legs have bristly spines at the top. These spines grind food and move it to the mouth as the crab walks. The last two legs end with "brushes." A horseshoe crab uses them like ski poles to push itself along.

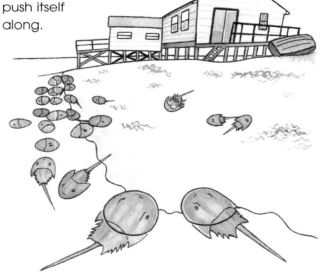

These crabs live on sand or mud from shallow to deep water. In spring and summer, they come on beaches to lay eggs. You can find horseshoe crabs from Maine to Florida and Texas.

Don't pick up horseshoe crabs by the tail—it hurts them.

BAY BARNACLE

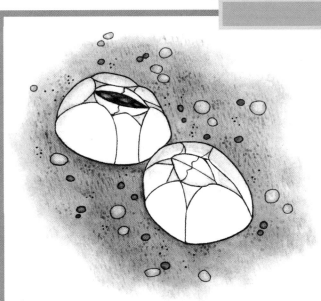

A bay barnacle is white. It is 1/4 inch high and 1/2 an inch wide. The shell has sharp edges.

When young, a barnacle glues its head to a rock, dock, shell or boat. It might even live on an animal like a horseshoe crab! A barnacle grows a hard white shell for a home. Overlapping shell plates form walls in the shape of a circle. At the top, four plates make a door. It opens like the petals of a flower. When closed, the door seals in water so the barnacle won't dry out.

Inside its shell, a barnacle is upside down. When it opens its doors, the barnacle sticks out six pairs of hairy legs. They sweep tiny floating plants and animals into the barnacle's mouth. Barnacles crowd together in their crusty homes. Sometimes younger barnacles live on top of older ones.

You can find bay barnacles in estuaries from Oregon to California, and from Nova Scotia, Canada to Florida and Texas.

SPECIAL WARNING

Stay away from coral reefs.

STRIPED SAND SOMETHING-OR-OTHER

Sand is washed on the beach one layer at a time. You can see this if you dig a deep hole. Sand layers look like stripes. Sand can slowly harden into stone. Sandstone has stripes, too.

WHAT YOU NEED

- a wide, clear glass jar with its lid (like a small peanut butter jar or baby food jar)

- sand—a bit more than the jar will hold

- food coloring in different colors

- 1/4 cup measure

- clean, wide plastic tubs—1 tub for each color of sand

- a tall plastic drink cup that fits easily inside the jar

- liquid glue

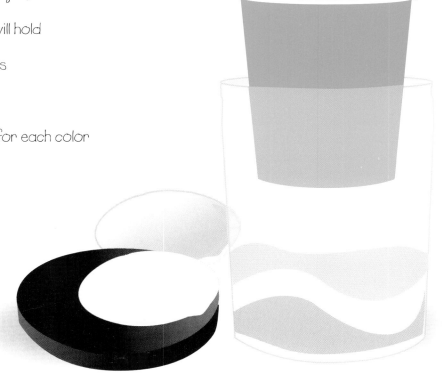

WHAT TO DO

▼

Your jar of striped sand can be a paperweight. Or you can just admire it on your dresser.

1 Put 1/4 cup of sand in a plastic tub. Add 8 to 10 drops of one food coloring. With a clean spoon, stir the sand and coloring. Make sure they are well mixed. Let the sand dry.

2 Repeat step 1 for each color of sand.

3 Pour colored sand from one of the tubs into the jar. Using the bottom of the plastic drink cup, press the sand down firmly. Add a different color of sand. Press it down firmly.

4 Add more layers of colored sand. Press each layer down before adding the next one. Fill the jar until sand is even with the top.

5 Put glue on the inside edge of the lid. Twist the lid on the jar. Let the glue dry.

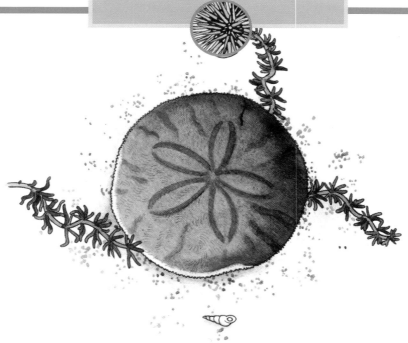

Sea stars and their relatives have spiny skin. They each have a body that can be divided into five parts. Sea stars, brittle stars and sea cucumbers can grow new body parts to replace lost ones. Urchins and sand dollars can repair holes in their skeletons.

All these animals have hard plates inside their skin. In urchins and sand dollars, the plates are joined in a rigid skeleton.

To move, most members of the sea star family pump seawater through their bodies into tube feet. When water is pumped out, the tube feet grip like suction cups and the animal pulls itself forward. A sea cucumber pumps body fluid instead of seawater into its tube feet.

Most spiny-skinned animals have no eyes. But sea stars have a red eyespot on the tip of each arm. They can see light and dark.

Sea vases belong to a group of animals called sea squirts. Sea anemones live attached to hard places and have poisonous stingers.

OCHRE SEA STAR

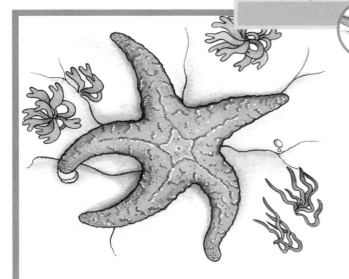

The ochre sea star likes to eat mussels. First it climbs onto a mussel. The tube feet stick to the mussel's shell. With its arms, it pulls the mussel open. Then the sea star pushes its stomach out through its mouth into the mussel. After eating it, the sea star pulls its stomach back inside.

Ochre (pronounced "O-KER") sea stars can climb straight up a rock wall. They can cling to rocks in crashing waves and open mussels.

This sea star is 20 inches across. It has 5 thick arms. On the underside are many little tube feet. Its mouth is in the center. Ochre is a yellow or reddish-yellow color. Ochre sea stars are yellow, orange, brown, red or purple and have short white spines.

The ochre sea star is found from Alaska to California. It lives on rocky shores pounded by waves. It is often found on mussel beds and in tide pools.

SPECIAL WARNING

Don't go out on rocks when waves are crashing.

DAISY BRITTLE STAR

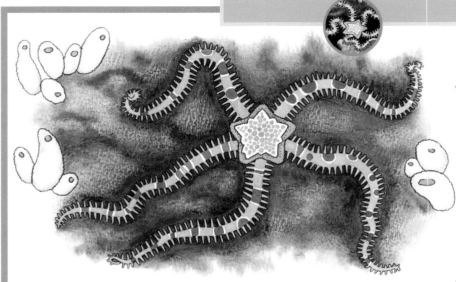

When scared, a brittle star waves its thin arms. It crawls away fast. It pulls itself along with one or two arms. The rest trail behind or push off the bottom. If something snags an arm, it breaks off easily. But the brittle star just grows a new one. This happens so often that their arms are usually different sizes.

The daisy brittle star has five long, skinny arms. The arms are about 4 inches long with fine, blunt spines. The brittle star's cookie-shaped body is about 1 inch across. Daisy brittle stars are spotted or striped. They can be red, orange, pink, yellow, white, blue, green, tan, brown, gray and black. They look like bright flowers. That's probably how they got their name.

A brittle star's arms are handy for catching small crabs or other food. It daintily stuffs them into its mouth underneath.

Daisy brittle stars hide under rocks in tide pools. They are found from Canada to Massachusetts, and from Alaska to California.

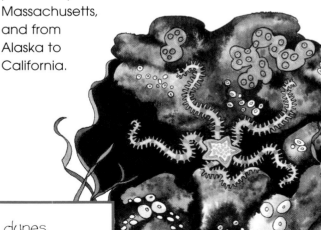

Stay off sand dunes.

PURPLE SEA URCHIN

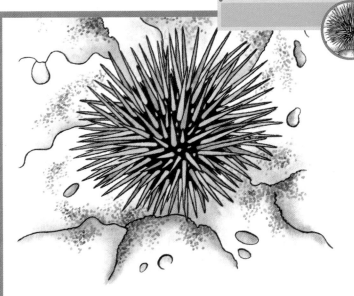

An urchin's mouth is underneath. It has five teeth that open and close like a beak. The purple sea urchin catches and eats floating seaweed with its tube feet. It also chews seaweed off rocks.

A sea urchin hides from enemies. It holds bits of shell and seaweed over itself with its tube feet. Or it may hide in a crack between rocks.

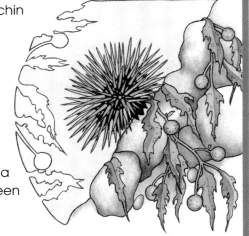

The purple sea urchin has spines all over. Among the spines are its tube feet. It looks like a porcupine. When an urchin walks with its tube feet, the spines act as stilts. It can move quickly. If an urchin turns over, its spines help it turn right side up.

A purple sea urchin is about 4 inches wide and 2 inches high. Its sharp spines are bright purple. Some kinds of urchins have poisonous spines, but not the purple urchin.

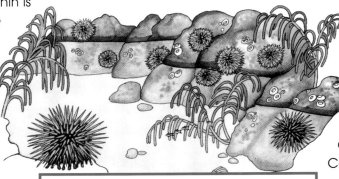

Groups of urchins live on rocks in shallow to deep water. They also live in tide pools. Purple sea urchins are found from British Columbia, Canada to California.

Don't pull off attached creatures. They will die.

167

ECCENTRIC SAND DOLLAR

The eccentric sand dollar is round and flat like a silver dollar. It has short, velvety spines that wiggle like grass waving in the wind. The spines help it burrow into sand.

The eccentric sand dollar is about 3 inches across and 1/2 inch thick. Its spines are lavender-gray, red-brown, brown or purple-black. On top, it has a five-point star with tiny holes around it. Tube feet stick out of the holes. On its underside are more tube feet.

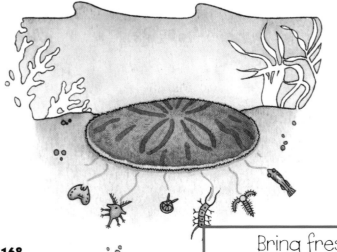

Thin grooves help guide food to its mouth in the center. The mouth has 5 small teeth that open and close like a beak. Sand dollars eat tiny plants and animals sifted from the sand. If you shake a sand dollar's skeleton, you'll hear the teeth rattling inside.

Eccentric sand dollars are found along the shoreline from Alaska to California. Groups of them burrow in the sand in shallow to deep water. Look in the sand for a flat track like a ribbon—a sand dollar may be buried where the track ends.

Bring fresh drinking water with you.

RED SEA CUCUMBER

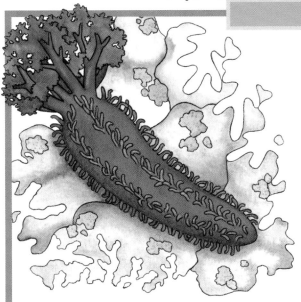

The red sea cucumber has two rows of tube feet on top. Three rows are underneath. It moves on these tube feet. Its muscles help push it slowly along.

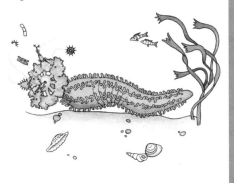

When attacked, a sea cucumber squirts out most of its insides! While the attacker eats these, the sea cucumber escapes. New insides soon grow back.

This creature's body is shaped like a cucumber. The skin is smooth but tough.

The red sea cucumber is about 10 inches long and 1 inch wide. It can be red, orange, pink or purple. At one end of its body is its mouth, with ten frilly orange feelers around it. Tiny floating plants and animals stick to the feelers. The sea cucumber pulls the feelers one by one into its mouth to eat the food.

This sea cucumber hides between rocks with its body curved so each end sticks out. They live in shallow water near the low-tide line. Red sea cucumbers can be found from Alaska to California.

Bring a flashlight for a night-time walk with an adult.

GIANT GREEN SEA ANEMONE

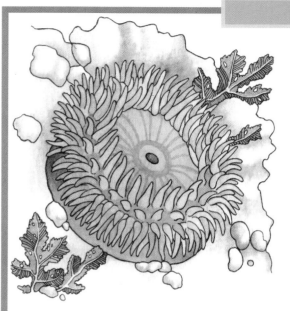

This sea anemone lives glued to rock. Sometimes dinner doesn't swim by for a long time. So, the anemone melts its glue and slowly glides to someplace new.

The giant green anemone can grow to be 12 inches high and 10 inches wide. The anemone's stalk is green-brown. The feelers are green, blue-green or white. The center is green, gray-green or blue-green.

Though it looks like a flower, the giant green sea anemone (pronounced "A-NEM-MEN-EE") is really an animal. Its body is a stalk, but petals aren't on top. Those are feelers with poisonous stingers. The feelers surround the anemone's mouth. When food swims near, the anemone stings it. Then the feelers pull the food down inside the anemone's mouth.

The giant green sea anemone lives along ocean and bay shores from Alaska to California. It is found on rocks and seawalls from above the low-tide line to deep water. It also lives in tide pools. When uncovered by the tide, giant green sea anemones close up to hold water inside.

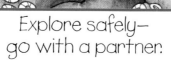

Explore safely—
go with a partner.

SEA VASE

A sea vase is about 6 inches high and 1 inch wide. It is pale yellow or green. You can see a sea vase's organs inside. On top, a sea vase has two short tubes close together. They are edged with yellow. A sea vase pumps water in one tube and out the other. It strains tiny plants and animals from the water to eat.

If you touch a sea vase, look out! It will squirt water at you. That's why this animal is also called a sea squirt. The sea vase has a body like a bag. It feels like plastic. Sand and other things may stick to its body. Seaweed often grows on it. On the bottom are bumps like roots. A young sea vase fastens its roots to a hard place.

Sea vases live on rocks, docks and boats in quiet bays. These animals live in shallow to deep water. You can find them from the Arctic to Rhode Island, and from Alaska to California.

Bring along this book and a magnifying glass.

SEASHORE TREASURE CHEST

You've found interesting things at the seashore. Now you're ready to set up your collection to show your friends.

WHAT YOU NEED

▼

- empty egg cartons or shoe boxes with lids
- cotton balls
- little pieces of paper for name tags
- pencil or pen
- scissors
- liquid glue

WHAT TO DO

▼

First, sort your seashore treasures by shape. Then follow these steps for each one:

1 Rinse off the seashell. If needed, carefully scrub it with an old, soft toothbrush.

2 While the seashell is drying, find out what it's called.

3 Write the name on a piece of paper. You can also put the date and place you found it.

4 Put cotton in an egg carton hole or on the bottom of a shoe box. Lay your object on top of the cotton.

5 Put a dot of glue on the back of the paper. Press it on the cotton beside the object.

Sea Star

Sand Dollar

Now your treasures won't get broken. And they're ready to show to your family and friends.

MAKE YOUR OWN SEASHELLS

You can make your own seashells to keep and decorate. Or you can give them away to friends so they can have "shells" of their own!

WHAT YOU NEED

- some seashells (shiny ones with bumps and ridges work best)

- modeling dough or clay that doesn't get hard

- a clean plastic tub (like an ice cream tub)

- an empty shoe box

- plaster of Paris and a stirring stick

- watercolors, paint, markers or crayons— anything you want to color them with

WHAT TO DO

1 Choose the shell you want to make first.

2 Knead the clay until it's soft.

3 Shape it into a smooth lump.

4 Press the bottom of the lump of clay into the box (to catch spills).

5 Place the shell on the clay like a cup (round side down).

6 Push the shell into the clay. Do not push all the way through to the box.

7 Carefully take the shell out of the clay.

8 Gently mix the plaster in the large plastic tub.

9 Slowly pour the wet plaster into the hole your shell made and fill it up.

10 Let the plaster dry at least 1 hour.

11 Carefully take the clay and plaster out of the box.

12 Pull the clay off the plaster.

13 Let the plaster dry at least 24 more hours.

SCRAPBOOK

Seashells, Crabs and Sea Stars

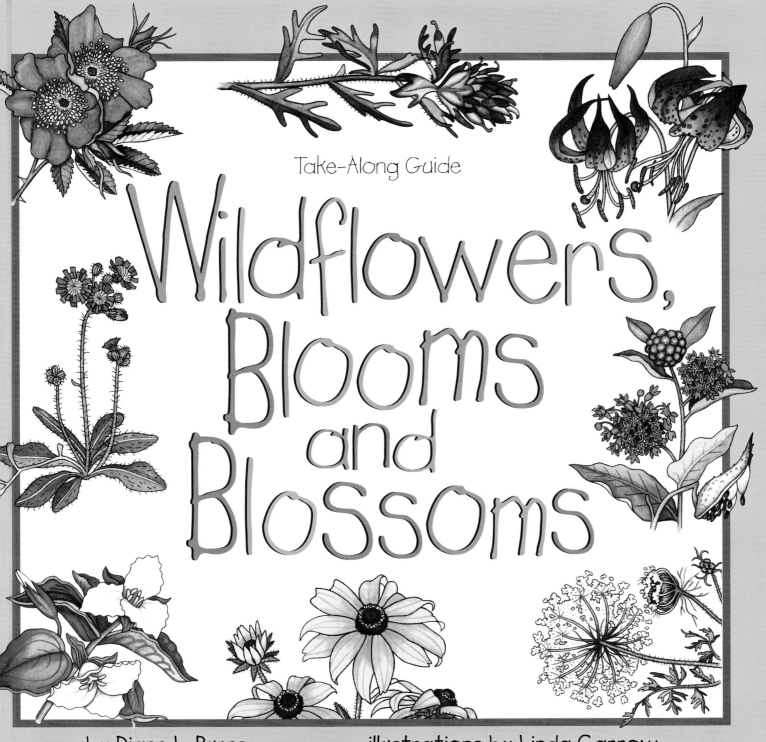

Take-Along Guide

Wildflowers, Blooms and Blossoms

by Diane L. Burns   illustrations by Linda Garrow

INTRODUCTION

Wildflowers are plants that grow freely. People do not choose where they grow. The plant does.

So, wildflowers grow in many different kinds of places. They are found in many colors, sizes and shapes. Some are beautiful. Some are plain-looking. Some smell good. Others do not.

Some wildflowers are native to the United States. Others were brought here by early settlers either on purpose or by accident.

Wildflowers have many kinds of seeds. Some are food for wildlife. The whole plant, or parts of it such as flowers, roots and leaves may also be food for certain birds and other animals.

This Take-Along Guide and its activities will help you find some interesting wildflowers. You can use the ruler on the back cover to measure what you discover. You can bring a pencil and draw what you see in the Scrapbook.

Have fun exploring the world of Wildflowers, Blooms and Blossoms!

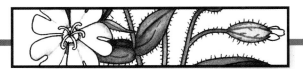

COMMON BUTTERCUP

WHAT IT LOOKS LIKE

Common buttercups grow to 3 feet tall and have many fuzzy branches.

The plant has two kinds of leaf stems and leaves. On the top, the small, three-part leaves have short stems or no stems at all. On the lower part of the plant, the leaf stems are long and each leaf is bigger and shaped like a skinny hand.

This wildflower's name comes from the delicate yellow cups that form the flowers. They are shallow, shiny, and about 1 inch across. Each flower has five overlapping petals that grow at the end of long, slender stems. It blooms from May through October.

INTERESTING FACTS

Because the plant can be poisonous to livestock, they avoid it.

WHERE TO FIND IT

The common buttercup likes wet meadows, swamps and road-sides. It grows in the western states, across the Plains states and to the Atlantic Coast.

Other kinds of buttercups grow in the south and central United States.

WHAT EATS IT

Ducks, wild turkeys and snow buntings eat buttercup seeds. Deer, muskrats and skunks eat the plants.

Wear boots and other protective clothing.

WHITE TRILLIUM

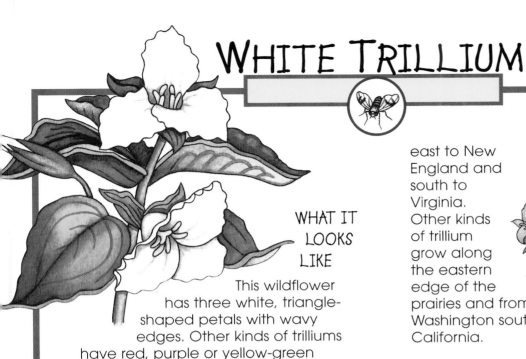

WHAT IT LOOKS LIKE

This wildflower has three white, triangle-shaped petals with wavy edges. Other kinds of trilliums have red, purple or yellow-green flowers. Each petal is about 3 inches long.

All trillium leaves grow in three's that look like smooth, dark green triangles. Each leaf is about 3 inches wide and 6 inches long.

This plant grows to 18 inches tall. It likes shaded, moist woods where it isn't bothered.

INTERESTING FACTS

Trillium is nicknamed "wake-robin," because it is said to wake the robins in the spring.

WHERE TO FIND IT

White trilliums grow from Minnesota and the Central Plains east to New England and south to Virginia. Other kinds of trillium grow along the eastern edge of the prairies and from Washington south to California.

White trilliums bloom in late spring. If you see a pink one, don't be fooled. After the white trillium's blossom has been open for a few days, it begins to turn pink.

WHAT EATS IT

Certain types of flies like the flowers, but probably not because of the smell. White trilliums have only the faintest of fragrance, and many others don't smell pleasant at all.

Please treat all wildflowers gently.

WILD LARKSPUR

WHAT IT LOOKS LIKE

Larkspur grows from less than 1 foot, to 8 feet tall, depending on the type.

The plant looks lacy because each larkspur leaf has several deep, finely cut sections. It looks like a skinny green hand.

The small flowers are often blue, but can also be white, pink or purplish with a pale center. Each flower has 5 petals. There is a long spur that sticks up from the top petal. They seem to nod gently as they bloom from spring, through summer and into fall.

The blossoms have a faint fresh scent.

WHERE TO FIND IT

Larkspur is found in woods and on slopes in much of the United States, especially in the Midwest and East. Shorter kinds grow in open, windy places. Taller ones grow in sheltered, moist places.

WHAT EATS IT

Hummingbirds like the flowers. It is harmful to cattle.

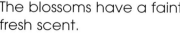

SPECIAL WARNING

INTERESTING FACTS

Some kinds of larkspur bloom high in the mountains—above 10,000 feet!

Caution! The seeds, which grow in the center of the flower, are poisonous.

182

TURK'S-CAP LILY

WHAT IT LOOKS LIKE

This sturdy wildflower grows to 8 feet tall! The upright stems are purplish. The narrow, sword-shaped leaves are about 5 inches long. They grow in groups along the stem.

Several orange-red flowers, speckled with brown spots, may grow at the end of the branch. They look graceful because the ends of the petals curl backward almost to the stem.

Turk's-cap petals are up to 3 inches long and less than 1 inch wide. At the base, each one is green, then yellowish spotted with brown, and orange-red at the tip.

WHERE TO FIND IT

The turk's-cap lily is found in the wet meadows and swampy woods of the eastern United States, west to the edge of the Great Plains.

It likes to be sheltered from harsh sun and wind. Look for it in July and August. One flower can bloom for a whole month. It does not have a smell.

WHAT EATS IT

Hummingbirds like the flowers.

INTERESTING FACTS

Their appearance, which looks like a middle-eastern hat, gives the flower its name.

Take your time and don't hurry.

BLACK-EYED SUSAN

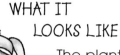

WHAT IT LOOKS LIKE

The plant grows to 3 feet tall on straight, stiff stems. Its few branches have fine hairs on them.

Black-eyed Susan leaves are thick, coarse and narrow. The bottom leaves, which are longer than the top ones, may be 2 inches wide and 7 inches long.

A single flower, up to 4 inches across, grows at the end of a stem or branch. Each flower has 12 or more bright yellow petals about 2 inches long. The center is a cone that looks like a big brown gumdrop.

pastures, roadsides and vacant lots across the United States.

It blooms from May through September and has a faint, sweet smell.

WHERE TO FIND IT

This wildflower and its relatives are sun-lovers. They thrive in dry meadows,

WHAT EATS IT

Cattle and sheep eat this wildflower.

INTERESTING FACTS

The Black-eyed Susan gets its name from the big, dark center in each flower.

184

Use the ruler on the back of this book to measure what you find.

PURPLE CONEFLOWER

WHERE TO FIND IT

The purple coneflower isn't fussy. It likes deep, moist soil, and can also grow in a dry, sunny spot. Look for it in the fields and meadows of the Midwest, and from Pennsylvania to Georgia, west to Oklahoma and north to Minnesota.

The flowers bloom from June to October, filling the air with their sweet scent.

WHAT IT LOOKS LIKE

The purple coneflower grows from 1 to 3 feet tall on a stout, hairy stem. There are only a few branches, if any.

Its narrow leaves are up to 6 inches long and 3 inches wide. They feel coarse and are hairy.

Purple coneflowers are huge drooping flowers. They grow up to 6 inches wide, at the tips of the stems and branches. Coneflower petals can be 3 inches long. They are found in bright purple, red, pink and white.

WHAT EATS IT

Goldfinches love these seeds!

INTERESTING FACTS

The dark center looks like a tiny, spiny beehive.

Sit quietly and you will see what kinds of wildlife also enjoy wildflowers.

BLOODROOT

WHAT IT LOOKS LIKE

This fragile plant grows no more than 1 foot tall on a smooth stem.

Each leaf looks hand-shaped and is about the same size. It is always curved with the whitish underneath part facing you.

A single white flower grows on a long stem separate from the leaves. It is as wide as 1-1/2 inches with a yellow center, and has as many as 16 petals. The white bud is often hidden inside the leaves, so you must look carefully to see it.

WHERE TO FIND IT

You will find bloodroot growing throughout much of the United States, especially in the Atlantic coastal states south to Florida, and west to Nebraska and Minnesota.

They bloom in rich shady woods from March to May, with no fragrance.

WHAT EATS IT

Bloodroot and ants help each other. Bloodroot's seeds are ant food. And bloodroot plants spread to new places because the ants carry the seeds with them.

SPECIAL WARNING

Caution! The juice is harmful. Do not swallow it!

186

BUTTER-AND-EGGS

WHAT IT LOOKS LIKE

Butter-and-eggs plants grow to 2-1/2 feet on thin stems that bend easily.

Soft, needle-shaped leaves, about as long as your finger, stick out along the length of the stem.

The showy yellow flowers blossom in a spike along the upper end of the branches. Each flower in the spike is about 1 inch long and looks like a set of small yellow lips with an orange center.

INTERESTING FACTS

This wildflower sounds like it might be someone's breakfast. But its name comes only from the flowers' coloring. The yellow outsides are the butter; the orange centers are the eggs.

WHERE TO FIND IT

Throughout the United States, butter-and-eggs grow in dry places, like vacant lots, where they often form large patches.

WHAT EATS IT

The many flowers on the butter-and-eggs plant bloom from July through October but their smell isn't pleasant. Still, bumblebees and some beetles like the pollen.

Tell an adult how long you will be gone.

187

CANADA THISTLE

WHAT IT LOOKS LIKE

Canada thistle plants can grow more than 4 feet tall. The straight, woody stems have slender green grooves in them.

Its narrow leaves can be longer than your hand. They have sharp spines.

Canada thistle flowers are purple, pink or yellow-white puffballs at the top of a green ball. They grow at the ends of the branches.

Each puffy flower, less than 1 inch wide, blooms all summer long and into autumn. They are very fragrant.

WHERE TO FIND IT

This wildflower could be nicknamed "survivor."

It is found across the United States almost everywhere a plant can grow.

In good conditions, it forms large patches in sunny vacant lots, meadows and overgrown fields.

WHAT EATS IT

Canada thistle is a special plant to goldfinches, which feed their young on the immature fruit. They also line their nests with the down from the flowers.

Bees and painted lady butterflies like Canada thistle flowers. Antelopes eat the whole plant. Goldfinches, sparrows and chickadees eat the mature seeds.

SPECIAL WARNING

Caution! Be careful of the sharp spines.

LATE GOLDENROD

WHAT IT LOOKS LIKE

Goldenrod blooms in an arch along the upper side of a short branch. About a dozen tiny yellow flowers form each arch. Look for them in late summer and early autumn and sniff for their sweet smell.

You might get a stiff neck finding this wildflower. Late goldenrod grows on a smooth, straight, purplish green stem that can be 8 feet tall!

Goldenrod leaves are narrow. They can be smooth on both sides, or hairy underneath. They grow along the stem and are about 6 inches long and 1 inch wide.

WHERE TO FIND IT

This is one of more than a hundred kinds of goldenrod that grow almost everywhere in the United States, in moist, sunny meadows.

Want to see next year's goldenrod now? Look in autumn, at the bottom of this year's goldenrod plant. You will find next year's stems already beginning to grow.

WHAT EATS IT

Flies, skippers and other butterflies like the flowers. Prairie chickens, rats and rabbits eat the leaves.

INTERESTING FACTS

Some kinds of goldenrod have latex in the leaves which scientists think may be a future source of rubber.

Take this book and a pencil when you go exploring.

189

Make a Wildflower Paperweight

Would you like to keep your favorite wild blossom? Make a wildflower paperweight! Besides keeping a pile of papers in place, the paperweight will keep your memory of sunny blooming meadows all year long.

WHAT YOU NEED

- A clean, smooth, fist-sized rock
- A freshly picked wildflower blossom, with or without its stem and leaf
- A bottle of white glue
- Hairspray or spray shellac

WHAT TO DO

1 Lay your wildflower wrong side up.

2 Carefully dab bits of white glue onto the back of the flower.

3 Paste the flower, right side up, to the rock. Work carefully, so the flower does not tear.

4 Allow the glue to dry before spraying the flower and the rock with hairspray or shellac. Be careful not to spray yourself!

5 Allow the spray to dry before you handle the paperweight.

You can display your creation in a favorite place, or give it as a gift.

something to do

Make a Friendship Band

Around the world, a gift of wildflowers has long been a symbol of friendship and trust. You can continue the tradition by making a wildflower friendship band.

WHAT YOU NEED
▼

- Long, freshly picked stems of wildflowers such as White Clover, Black-eyed Susan, Ox-eye Daisy, Indian Paintbrush, Orange Hawkweed, Butter-and-Eggs, Late Goldenrod, Evening Lychnis or Queen Anne's Lace.
- You can use the stems with or without the leaves and flowers attached.

Be sure to use very fresh green stems. And your plant band may last for several days.

WHAT TO DO
▼

1 Tie together three stems of approximately the same length.
2 Gently braid the stems together.
3 When you reach the other end, tie it carefully.
4 Hold the braid around your wrist, ankle or forehead.
5 Tie it into a circle at the proper length.

Your plant band is much like the ones long-ago people wore on special occasions. You can keep it, or give it to a friend.

CORNFLOWER

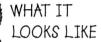

WHAT IT LOOKS LIKE

Cornflower plants grow to about 2 feet tall. The stems are slender, grooved and branched. The many gray-green leaves can be woolly when young. They look like grass and are about 6 inches long.

Each flower is really a cluster of mini-flowers with the ones on the outer edge bigger than the center ones. They have deeply toothed edges.

The round flower blooms at the end of each branch. It is between 1 and 2 inches wide and tall. It is usually deep bright blue, but can also be purple, pink or white.

WHERE TO FIND IT

Cornflowers like fields, vacant lots and roadsides from New England south to Virginia and west across the United States to the Pacific Northwest.

Cornflowers, which do not have a smell, bloom in late summer and early autumn.

WHAT EATS IT

Wildlife do not usually eat the cornflower.

INTERESTING FACTS

This wildflower's nickname is "bachelor's button" because the blossom's ragged edges once reminded people of the frayed cloth buttons worn by "helpless bachelors."

Visit your favorite wildflowers in different seasons to see how they grow and change.

WHITE CLOVER

WHAT IT LOOKS LIKE

White clover stems may be up to 3 feet long, but they grow along the ground. Runners send down roots at each joint. The stems on which leaves and flowers grow are only about 5 inches tall.

Small and green, clover leaves always grow in groups of three or sometimes four. Each has a pale triangle across it. The leaves grow on stems separate from the flowers.

White clover flowers are small white to pink-white globes that bloom from May to December. They have a sweet smell.

WHERE TO FIND IT

Some type of white clover is found growing nearly everywhere in the United States, in lawns and fields and along roadsides.

WHAT EATS IT

Sulphur butterflies especially like clover flowers. Deer, squirrels, marmots, rabbits and grouse eat white clover leaves.

INTERESTING FACTS

Many people think four-leaf clovers are lucky. This idea started long ago when people believed that whoever found one would be able to see witches.

To see small plants more easily, carry a plastic magnifying glass with you.

WILD ROSE

WHAT IT LOOKS LIKE

This wildflower grows from 1 to 5 feet tall on straight stems that often have prickles. The plant can look slim or bushy, depending on what kind of wild rose it is and where it is growing.

Rose leaves are small, oval and dark green. Several stems usually grow into a bush.

The flowers can be as big as the palm of your hand. They are pink, white, yellow or red and grow singly or in a cluster. Each flower has a yellow center.

Its thorny patches make good hiding places for many animals, such as rabbits, mice and grouse. Wild rose bushes even make good homes for birds like cedar waxwings and chipping sparrows that nest in the thorny branches.

WHERE TO FIND IT

The wild rose likes sunny dry places such as rocky roadsides, fencelines and pastures. It grows almost everywhere in the United States.

It blooms from June to September. You can find the flowers by the strong, sweet smell.

WHAT EATS IT

Birds and other animals that eat the fruit, called hips, are grouse, quail, wild turkey, squirrels, mice, bear, mountain sheep, opossum and coyote. Deer and antelope eat the twigs and leaves. Rabbits chew the buds and the bark. Bees like the flowers.

INTERESTING FACTS

Rose hips, which have more vitamin C than oranges, can be found on the bush all winter.

Watch where you step.

BUSHY ASTER

WHAT IT LOOKS LIKE

The bushy aster grows to about 3 feet tall. The stems are widely branched, slender and tough. The green leaves are about as long as your finger and very narrow.

Bushy aster flowers grow in clusters. Each one is small, about 1/2 inch across, with thin, narrow petals. The flowers are blue-white to white, with yellow centers.

The flowers bloom in late summer and early fall without a smell. They can even be found on the plant after the first snowfall.

Other kinds of aster grow in almost any kind of soil, from rocky to boggy, and are found across the United States.

Interesting Facts

The bushy-looking top gives the plant its name. Some kinds of aster grow to 8 feet tall.

WHERE TO FIND IT

The bushy aster grows across the eastern and midwestern United States, in sandy soil.

WHAT EATS IT

Some kinds of wild aster are good food for elk and deer. Other kinds make some animals sick. Bees, flies and butterflies like the flowers.

Never pull up wildflowers by the roots. They cannot grow back.

MARSH MARIGOLD

WHAT IT LOOKS LIKE

This wildflower grows to 2 feet tall on thick, smooth stems.

Marsh marigold leaves are dark green and heart-shaped. They are smooth, from 2 to 8 inches wide.

These flowers have no special smell. They are bright yellow and shaped like a waxy shallow cup. Each one is less than 2 inches across. The centers are yellow-green.

The flowers open and close with the sun while they bloom from April to June.

WHERE TO FIND IT

This plant likes wet areas. It is found in swamps, marshes and ditches with slow-moving or standing water.

Marsh marigolds grow throughout New England and the East Coast, south to South Carolina and west to Nebraska. They are also found on the West Coast.

WHAT EATS IT

No wildlife eats this plant because it is harmful to them.

INTERESTING FACTS

Marsh marigolds were once used as a sign of spring. Long-ago people hung bunches of the wildflower over their doorways on May Day.

SPECIAL WARNING

Caution! Don't eat this plant! It can make a person sick.

WILD BLUE FLAG

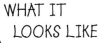

WHAT IT LOOKS LIKE

This plant grows to 3 feet tall. Its stems are straight and may have a branch or two that reach upward.

The blue flag's leaves are narrow, like an upright sword.

Its flowers often grow two to a stem. They are violet-blue, with streaks of yellow, white and green. Several slender petals curve gracefully downward. Each one is about 4 inches long.

WHERE TO FIND IT

This wildflower grows along the marshy edges of meadows, and open wet brushland that is sunny. Look for it among other wet-loving plants, not in a patch by itself.

One kind or another of blue flag grows nearly everywhere in the United States. They bloom from May to July.

WHAT EATS IT

The leaves provide hiding places to wild ducks and geese, but the wild flag plant is not a wildlife food, except that hummingbirds like the flowers which have a faint, fresh scent.

INTERESTING FACTS

The root of one kind of blue flag is used to make perfume.

Never collect rare or endangered wildflowers.

FIREWEED

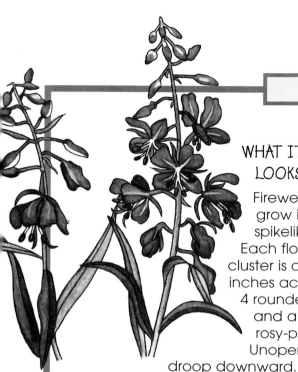

WHAT IT LOOKS LIKE

Fireweed flowers grow in a spikelike cluster. Each flower in the cluster is about 1-1/2 inches across, with 4 rounded petals and a bright, rosy-purple color. Unopened buds droop downward.

This wildflower can grow to 8 feet, although most are 3 to 5 feet tall. Each stem is straight and strong. It can be smooth or have a fine downy covering. It is branched or unbranched.

Fireweed leaves are dark green on top, pale green underneath. They are pointed, and each is about 6 inches long and 1 inch wide.

WHERE TO FIND IT

Fireweed is found in the United States from New England to South Carolina and west to California and Alaska. It also grows from the Rocky Mountains south into Arizona.

The flowers bloom in summer months, with the lower flowers on the plant blossoming first.

Look for it in open areas and along sunny roadsides.

WHAT EATS IT

Although the flowers have no smell, hummingbirds and bees like them. Deer and moose eat the plant. Chipmunks eat the seeds.

INTERESTING FACTS

Fireweed got its name because it likes to grow in places after a fire. And from a distance, fields of open blooms look as if they are on fire.

Take sunscreen with you, and water to drink.

QUEEN ANNE'S LACE

WHAT IT LOOKS LIKE

This wildflower grows 4 to 5 feet tall on a strong, slender stem. The leaves are feathery and look like carrot tops.

Each large flower is made up of many smaller ones. The large blossom can be 4 inches wide, and up to 2 inches thick. It is white and can have a purple or reddish flowerette in the center.

The flowers of Queen Anne's Lace take two years to bloom. The first year, there are no flowers, only a circle of ferny leaves and its root. In the second year, the plant blooms between June and September.

After it blooms, the flower folds inward into a "nest" that shelters the plant's fruits. Look for this in early autumn.

WHERE TO FIND IT

Queen Anne's Lace is a common wildflower in sunny places like roadsides, vacant lots and fields. Though it is more common in the eastern United States, it can be found from coast to coast.

WHAT EATS IT

Sweet-smelling Queen Anne's Lace flowers are enjoyed by bees, butterflies, moths and flies. Its seeds are food for moles and grouse. Moles also eat the roots.

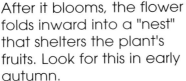

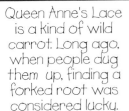

INTERESTING FACTS

Queen Anne's Lace is a kind of wild carrot. Long ago, when people dug them up, finding a forked root was considered lucky.

SPECIAL WARNING

Caution! Some people's skin is sensitive to touching the wet leaves of Queen Anne's Lace.

199

OX-EYE DAISY

WHAT IT LOOKS LIKE

Ox-eye daisies can grow to 3 feet tall. The green, straight stem is smooth and usually unbranched.

Its narrow leaves can be 3 inches long. They are dark shiny green.

Each flower, up to 2 inches wide, grows at the end of a branch, one to a stem. There are 20 to 30 flat white petals, usually with a dent or two in the end of each petal. The flower's yellow center is depressed in the middle, like a thumbprint.

WHERE TO FIND IT

Ox-eyes grow from coast to coast, though they are less common in the West and South. These daisies like sunny roadsides, pastures and fields.

They have no smell, and bloom from May through November.

This daisy is named for its flowers, which reminded pioneer settlers of the large, gentle eyes of their oxen. These pioneers brought the daisy with them from their native countries.

WHAT EATS IT

Wildlife do not usually eat the ox-eye daisy.

Get permission before going onto someone's land.

PICKERELWEED

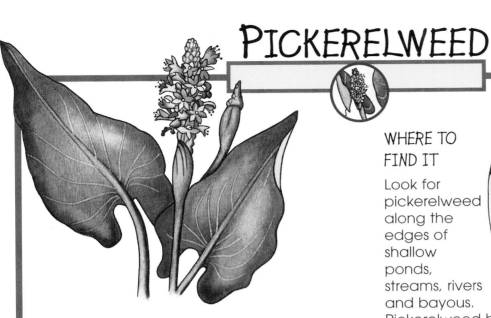

WHERE TO FIND IT

Look for pickerelweed along the edges of shallow ponds, streams, rivers and bayous. Pickerelweed blooms all summer and into early fall.

It grows throughout the eastern United States west to Minnesota and south to the Gulf of Mexico, Florida and Texas.

WHAT IT LOOKS LIKE

Pickerelweed can grow to 4 feet tall. Its thick, dark green leaves are smooth, wide, and shaped like spears. They grow up from the base and can be 10 inches long and 6 inches wide.

Pickerelweed often forms a thick, matted bed of leaves and flowers.

The pale blue to deep violet flower spike is about 4 inches long. It grows at the end of a thick stem. The flower clump is crowded with small, individual flowers that have no smell.

INTERESTING FACTS

This wildflower gets its name because it often grows at the edge of water in which the pickerel fish is found.

WHAT EATS IT

The seeds are food for ducks and deer. The plant is food for muskrats.

Never step into water without first knowing how deep it is.

201

Preserve a Wildflower

Fresh blooms and blossoms wilt and fade once they are picked. Pressing each one to remove moisture preserves them much longer.

WHAT YOU NEED

▼

- A freshly picked wildflower with a flat blossom, such as buttercup, daisy, cornflower, wild rose or bushy aster. (Thicker blooms do not press well.) You can leave the stem and a leaf attached.

- 2 flat, smooth bricks (or big and heavy books)

- 2 pieces of waxed paper cut to fit the size and shape of the bricks or books

- 2 pieces of paper towel to fit the size and shape of the bricks or books

WHAT TO DO

▼

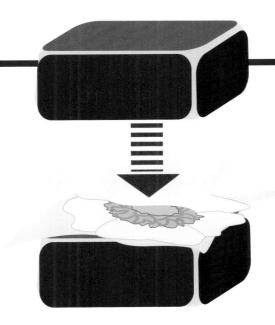

1. Lay a piece of waxed paper on top of one brick (or book). Then lay a piece of paper towel on top.
2. Next, place the wildflower.
3. Put the second piece of paper towel on top of the flower. Then lay the second piece of waxed paper over it all.
4. Finally, lay the second brick or book on top of your "sandwich."
5. Leave the whole "sandwich" alone for a few weeks while the flower dries and is pressed by the weight of the bricks.
6. Then, carefully take off the top brick or book.
7. Peel away the waxed paper and paper towel from both sides of the pressed wildflower.

You can keep the pressed flower as a memento in a favorite book or use it to make other things.

Here are some ideas:

- Glue it to plain paper and make your own sheets of wildflower stationery.
- Glue it to plain folded paper and make your own greeting cards.
- Press it between strips of clear tape to make a bookmark.
- Press it between strips of clear tape to make a suncatcher, and hang it in your window.
- Glue it to a safety pin for a beautiful piece of jewelry.

Pressed and preserved wildflowers make great gifts!

WILD COLUMBINE

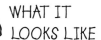

WHAT IT LOOKS LIKE

Wild columbine is a short, lacy-looking bush that can grow 2 feet tall.

Its dark green leaves have deeply cut edges and grow in groups. They are lighter green underneath. Each leafy group can be as wide as 8 inches.

Each blossom is a drooping red and yellow bell. It nods at the end of the stem and is 1 to 2 inches long. The flower looks like a hollow, round honeycomb with 5 long spurs behind.

It blooms from April through July.

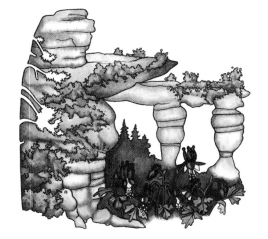

shade along rocky cliffs, fields and fencelines.

This wildflower is found across the eastern and central United States, south to Florida and Texas, and into the Rocky Mountains.

WHERE TO FIND IT

Columbines like rich woods and loose soil. Look for them growing in light

WHAT EATS IT

Even though this flower is not fragrant, it is a favorite of moths and butterflies.

INTERESTING FACTS

Sometimes bumblebees steal the sweet nectar without touching the flower to pollinate it.

204

Stay safe! Don't go near the edges of cliffs and outcroppings.

CHICORY

WHAT IT LOOKS LIKE

Chicory plants grow to 4 feet tall and look bare. The tough clump of hollow stems is hairy and branched. The stems start out green, turn purple, then red and finally brown as summer ends.

The few, skinny leaves along the stem can be 6 inches long. They have deep cuts in the edges and are gray-green. Most of the leaves grow in a circle at the base of the stem.

Chicory's flowers bloom along the upper stems. Each head is about the size of a quarter. Several flowers may be clustered together, right against the stem. They are usually blue, but they can also be pink or white.

The tips of the petals are square with notches. Each flower looks fringed and has no smell.

WHERE TO FIND IT

Chicory likes sunny fields, roadsides and vacant lots throughout the United States.

It blooms from July through October.

WHAT EATS IT

Some people cook chicory as a vegetable. Some use the root to make a hot drink like coffee.

Be aware of changing weather.

WILD LILY OF THE VALLEY

WHAT IT LOOKS LIKE

Wild lily of the valley plants grow about 6 inches tall on a zig-zag stem.

There are usually 2 leaves, sometimes 3, spaced along the stem. They are about as long as your finger. The heart-shaped end wraps around the stem. The other end is pointed.

The white flowers form a small, starry cluster. Each flower has 4 petals, each less than 1/4 inch long and wide. They have no smell.

WHERE TO FIND IT

The plant likes moist woods and brushy areas where the soil is loose and deep. It often forms a dense mat, especially under trees.

Look for it in the midwestern United States eastward to the Atlantic coast and south to Georgia. The flowers bloom from May to July.

WHAT EATS IT

Chipmunks, mice and grouse eat the pale, speckled berries. Rabbits eat the plants.

INTERESTING FACTS

This wildflower is sometimes known as "mayflower" because the plant blooms in springtime.

Stay away from poison ivy and poison oak when you explore.

ORANGE HAWKWEED

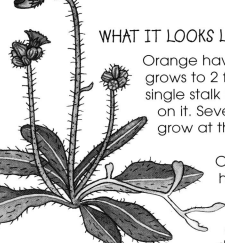

WHAT IT LOOKS LIKE

Orange hawkweed grows to 2 feet tall. The single stalk has dark hair on it. Several blooms grow at the very top.

Orange hawkweed flowers have yellow centers with a deep orange fringe around the outside. The petals look square, with blunt ends that are ragged. The whole flower looks fringed. It is about the size of a nickel.

The leaves, which are hairy and coarse, grow only in a circle at the base of the stem. They are about the size of your thumb.

fields, meadows, roadsides and lawns. They bloom from summer through early autumn.

When several hawkweed buds are open on the stalk, the plant has a sweet smell.

WHAT EATS IT

Grouse and wild turkeys eat the leaves and seeds. Deer, rabbits and mountain sheep eat the plants.

INTERESTING FACTS

Some people call this plant "devil's paintbrush" because it sometimes grows where people don't want it to grow.

WHERE TO FIND IT

There are about 50 different kinds of hawkweeds that grow across the United States in

When gathering common wildflowers, take only what you need and leave the others.

EVENING LYCHNIS

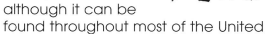

WHAT IT LOOKS LIKE

Evening lychnis flowers look like a green-striped, or purple-striped bag with petals sticking out of the closed top. Each single white flower, with its 5 deeply notched petals, grows at the end of each branched stem. There are 5 threads that poke up from the center.

The plant is hairy and the stems are slender. It grows from 1 to 2 feet tall with thin, sticky branches going every which way.

Its downy green leaves close around the stem and make a point at the other end. They are small and slender, about 2 inches long. The undersides are paler green than the tops.

WHERE TO FIND IT

Evening lychnis is widespread across the eastern United States, although it can be found throughout most of the United States. It likes places like vacant lots and roadsides.

These flowers are closed during the day. They have a faint, fresh scent. Look for the blossoms all summer and into early fall.

WHAT EATS IT

Sparrows eat the seeds. Moths like the flowers.

INTERESTING FACTS

Evening lychnis blossoms open at night when moths can pollinate them.

When exploring at night, take a flashlight.

PURPLE LOOSESTRIFE

WHAT IT LOOKS LIKE

Each clump of straight, purple (or spiked) loosestrife stems grows from 1-1/2 to 4 feet tall.

The sword-shaped leaves are wide at the base and narrow at the top. They are covered with fine hair and grow in pairs around the stem.

This loosestrife grows flowers in a purple spike. Each small flower in the spike has 6 skinny, curved petals. They do not have a smell. Other kinds of purple loosestrife grow their flowers along the stem.

WHERE TO FIND IT

Purple loosestrife likes moist places, choosing the shores of lakes and rivers, wet meadows, and ditch edges. It grows from New England south to Virginia, west to Missouri and north to Minnesota.

Loosestrife blooms during mid-summer and early fall.

WHAT EATS IT

Ground squirrels eat the seeds.

INTERESTING FACTS

It is banned in some states because it takes over the growing space other wildflowers need to survive.

Pay attention to everything around you.

COMMON MILKWEED

WHAT IT LOOKS LIKE

Milkweeds grow to 5 feet tall, and usually have just 1 stem per plant.

The leathery, oval leaves of the common milkweed are smooth and about 6 inches long and 4 inches wide. They are fuzzy underneath.

The flowers look rubbery. Each clump is about the size of a golf ball, and can be white, red-orange or pink-violet.

WHERE TO FIND IT

These plants don't like to be crowded by other kinds of wildflowers. Instead, they usually grow by themselves in a patch. Some kinds of milkweed grow almost everywhere across the United States.

They may be found in fields, meadows, woods or swamps, or along roadsides. You can find them blooming from early to late summer.

WHAT EATS IT

This is a special plant to Monarch butterflies. Some birds also eat milkweed seeds. Antelopes eat the plants. Spicy, sweet-smelling milkweed flowers attract flies, bees and butterflies.

INTERESTING FACTS

This wildflower gets its name from the milky juice in its sturdy stems.

Tell an adult where you are going, or take one with you.

VIRGINIA BLUEBELL

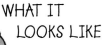

WHAT IT LOOKS LIKE

Virginia bluebells grow from 1 to 2 feet tall on smooth stems.

Virginia bluebell leaves are yellow-green and oval. They are smooth and can be longer than your hand.

The plant is named for its small bell-shaped flowers. They are blue, about 1 inch long, and grow in clusters.

The blossoms have a faint, fresh scent while they are blooming in April and May.

WHERE TO FIND IT

They like rich soil and shady places, such as the woods near rivers and other bottomlands. Look for Virginia bluebells in the eastern United States and along the upper Great Lakes as far west as northern Minnesota.

WHAT EATS IT

Wildlife do not usually eat Virginia bluebells.

INTERESTING FACTS

Look closely at the buds. The flowers are blue, but the buds are pink!

Never hurt any wildflowers with your hands or tools.

INDIAN PAINTBRUSH

WHAT IT LOOKS LIKE

Indian paintbrush flowers are small. Each one looks like an upended paintbrush covered with red and yellow color. The flower grows at the end of the stem.

Each flower is really a group of short, 2-lipped flowers that are yellow-green. You can easily see the taller, 3-part sections that are tipped with red. The yellow-green flowers are nearly hidden beneath them.

The stem is hairy and straight. The few leaves along its length are shaped like thin, bristly pitchforks. They are about 2 inches long.

There is also a circle of leaves around the base of the plant on the ground. These are oval and up to 3 inches long.

WHERE TO FIND IT

This wildflower grows from 1 to 2 feet tall in vacant lots, roadsides and meadows. It is found throughout the eastern United States, south to the Gulf Coast and west into the Great Plains.

They bloom during late spring and early summer. They have no smell.

WHAT EATS IT

Deer and wild mules eat the plants. Hummingbirds enjoy the flowers.

INTERESTING FACTS

Although they have good roots, they sometimes attach themselves to other plant roots for easy food.

Don't approach or touch any wild animals you may see.

JOHNNY JUMP-UP

WHAT IT LOOKS LIKE

Some of these plants are hairy, others are smooth. They can be as tall as 1 foot, but the stems prefer to hug the ground.

The leaves may be small and round, often shaped like small spoons. On other jump-ups, the leaves may be notched, or heart-shaped.

Johnny jump-up flowers are violet, blue, yellow and white. The 6 petals are arranged like a small face. They are scattered at all levels of the plant.

WHERE TO FIND IT

This wildflower grows throughout the eastern United States and into the Midwest. Look for it in meadows, shady wooded edges, and along streambanks and roadsides.

Freshly opened flowers may have a faint scent, but it does not last. They bloom from late spring through early autumn.

WHAT EATS IT

The seeds are eaten by mourning doves, quail and grouse. The roots are liked by wild turkeys.

Don't drop any litter.

Make a Container Rainbow

No matter where you live, you can plant and enjoy a rainbow of color.

WHAT YOU NEED

- A clean, empty ice cream bucket with a few holes punched in the bottom.
- Good garden soil to fill it.
- Seeds of any of the short, easy-to-grow wildflowers in this book, such as johnny jump-up, orange hawkweed, coneflower and white clover.
- A watering can.

Butterflies love plants such as milkweed, wild rose and Queen Anne's Lace. You will be amazed how quickly they come when the flowers begin to bloom!

WHAT TO DO

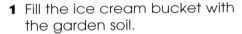

1 Fill the ice cream bucket with the garden soil.

2 Lightly press the wildflower seeds into the soil. Remember that in the wild, seeds often lay near the top of the ground.

3 Water the top of the soil to moisten it. Do not make it soggy.

4 Set the bucket in a warm, sunny place. Water the soil as needed to keep it moist.

5 After a few weeks, the seeds should sprout. Continue to water the bucket as the seeds grow into a rainbow of flowers for you to enjoy.

If you have a place outdoors, you can plant a wildflower garden to attract butterflies. A sunny, unused corner of your yard or garden works very well. It can be as big or little as you wish.

SCRAPBOOK

Wildflowers, Blooms and Blossoms

My Nature Adventures

The date of my adventure: _____

The people who came with me: _____

_____

Where I went: _____

What I saw:

_____

_____

_____

_____

The date of my adventure: _____

The people who came with me: _____

_____

Where I went: _____

What I saw:

_____

_____

_____

_____

My Nature Adventures

The date of my adventure: _____

The people who came with me: _____

_____

Where I went: _____

What I saw:

_____   _____

_____   _____

_____   _____

_____   _____

The date of my adventure: _____

The people who came with me: _____

_____

Where I went: _____

What I saw:

_____   _____

_____   _____

_____   _____

_____   _____

More Fun With Nature Index